"...Micki Moore is sleek, sexy and sophisticated....She has a sense of humour and intelligence."

— *The Gazette*

"...an autobiographical how-to manual written staccato style, mixing down-to-earth humor and anecdotal intimacy...devoted to women being themselves...in their battle for survival and success..."

— *The Record*

"<u>Making It</u> has instant appeal..."

— *The Examiner*

making it

making it

Getting What You Want: Love, Sex, Career, Family, and Self

by **Micki Moore**

with **Helen Bullock**

A Dell Book

Published by
Dell Distributing, A Division of Doubleday Canada Limited
105 Bond St.
Toronto, Ontario
M5B 1Y3

ISBN 0-440-15452-9

Reprinted by arrangement with Methuen Publications
Printed in Canada by Gagne Printers Ltd.
First Dell printing — March 1986

To the loves of my life:
Leonard, Lance, and Lisa

Contents

Don't Put Up with Put-Downs
Getting Tough
Action Defeats Fear
Intimidation
The Art of Negotiation

Four / Having It All—Is It Possible?

Micki's "Somebody-Something" Theory
Career and Love: Do Passionate Pursuits Detract from
    One Another?
Two out of Three Ain't Bad
Three out of Three: Hello, Superwoman!
Shifting Priorities: Maybe That's What You Wanted Five
    Years Ago
What Really Makes You Happy?

Five / Don't Talk About It, Do It!

Stop Putting Your Life on Hold
Whatever Happened to Your Dreams?
What's Holding You Back?
There Is No Failure, Only Experience to Grow From
The Best Chance of Getting What You Want Is Knowing
    What It Is
Get the Action Habit
Motivation: What Makes You Run?
When Preparation Meets Opportunity
Improper Channels
Don't Go into the Boxing Ring without Your Gloves On
The Truth about Success

Six / Men: Making the Connection

Can't Live with Them, Can't Live without Them
What Do You Want in a Man?
What Do Men Want?

**making it**

Introduction

I will never be a little old lady in a rocking chair talking about what I should have done and could have done. I have lived my dreams.

Looking back, I have to laugh. I used to be so shy I would write out my half of a conversation before making a telephone call. I spoke with a thick, high-pitched Southern accent. To me, it's nothing short of a miracle that years later I make my living, in fact, from my voice (two years of elocution and diction, thank you), conversing spontaneously on television with world-renowned experts and celebrities.

Yet it wasn't a miracle, really. I wasn't born with any special talent; whatever I've accomplished or acquired has come from sheer hard work, determination, a kind of blind naiveté, and the willingness to take risks. I'm afraid I can't even hang my hat on that old standby, luck. Nothing ever seemed to just happen to me; I had to plant the seeds and make it happen.

I have lived many lives; being in front of the camera was just one of them. I have been a wife, mother, home-maker, working woman, single parent, and co-vivant. I have worked as a cashier, model, art gallery tourer, researcher, news reporter, actress, writer, and television interviewer. (I've even been the voice of a shredded wheat!!)

I have traveled the world; I have lived and worked in New York, London, England, and Toronto. I have done it all, and I still have more to do.

Having lived as both a married woman and a single woman (in that order) and having raised two children, I truly understand the struggle of most women to achieve emotional and financial independence. And what it means to come full circle, finding a healthy and positive love and interdependence with a very special man. I know what it means to want and "have it all."

I think that success is the journey and not the destination. And a successful life is knowing how to get the most out of that journey: savoring each day, going after what you want, overcoming obstacles, growing and changing, and striving to be the best you can be.

I've traveled a long distance in a short time, and this is what I've learned along the way . . .

I

Making It

● *Build Yourself from the Inside Out*

My moment had come. I got the call.

CITY-TV in Toronto was looking for a host for their new afternoon talk show. Would I come down and audition?

WOULD I?!?!

Would I? I only had callouses on both fists from pounding the doors of every television station in town trying to get my own show.

The assignment: Co-host a live show with two of the station's male personalities. There was nothing to prepare—do a couple of interviews, a couple of commentaries—wing it, so to speak.

On audition day I put on my lucky red dress—and slipped a black grease pencil up my sleeve. Armed with a bit of trendy pop psychology from my files about men and mustaches, I was ready to make my mark.

As the cameras rolled, I glided through my interviews and commentaries. I filled in the dead spaces with visual chitchat by drawing mustaches on my co-hosts and giving them a psychological rundown: Men with walrus mustaches wear boxer shorts, have false teeth, prefer oral sex, and are Capricorns. Those with handlebars are usually bald, into S and M, smoke a pipe, and are Libras (real heavy-duty stuff out of the back pages of *Cosmo*).

The kicker came just before the wrap-up, when I

1

penciled a Don Ameche special on my own upper lip!

Can you imagine the conversation as the executives screened the twenty or so audition tapes? There I was going through my paces in a frilly red dress and sporting a hairy upper lip. WHO IS THAT BABE!

My "Skills-Plus" theory worked—do the best job you can, but make sure they won't forget you. They didn't. A memo went out: "Get me the girl with the mustache!"

I did it!

And I deserved it. At the age of thirty-seven, with eighteen years of pounding pavements, endless commercials, voice-overs, bit parts, Grade D movies, tryouts, and walk-ons, my dream had come true—I had my own TV talk show.

My kids shared my new notoriety in diverse ways.

My ever-enterprising son Lance took to the streets one day when I was sunbathing in the backyard. "Come one, come all, see Micki Moore in a bikini." Ever the businessman, even in short pants, he sold tickets for twenty-five cents a peek!

Sleepy from the sun, I opened my eyes to see eight little boys between the ages of four and ten, having coughed up their allowance, staring down at me. Before I could speak, one junior Hugh Hefner with a froggy voice who was staring beadily at my chest croaked, "Mrs. Moore, them sure are nice." The next day, this Don Juan rang my doorbell and asked, "Mrs. Moore, wanna come out and play?"

Daughter Lisa went to the other extreme. She found her mother's new fame an utter embarrassment to her adolescent soul.

"Mother," she begged, "promise me that when my friends come over you won't come into the room, you won't say anything. Mother, promise me you'll stay upstairs."

One night I agreed to pick Lisa and her friends up from a dance. "Mother," she wailed, "please promise me you won't come into the dance. Just stay in the car."

What mother could resist such anguished pleas? So I waited in the car ... with a garbage bag over my head. Peering out of the two little eye slits, I thought: I know loved ones have a difficult time adjusting to success, but this is ridiculous!

There I was, hiding in a garbage bag, repeating to myself, "I am a successful television personality, and I am *making it*." And I *was* making it, making it as a human being, and I believe that's what counts.

Not casks of jewels, not wall-to-wall mink, not half a dozen husbands or my name and face on every billboard—these are not the ways I measure success.

I look at my work and I think: Micki, you are a professional success.

I look at my children, Lance and Lisa, now independent young adults, and I think: Micki, you have made it as a mother.

I look at Leonard, my one and only, with whom I've lived for three years, through the reconciling of two grown-up families (my two kids, his three), through two demanding careers, the death of the family dog, and the birth of two budgies, and I think: Micki, you have made it in love, too!

How about you? Do you long for a little more in your life?

Let's do a quick rundown on *you*:

- Are you basically an intelligent, hardworking, loving woman who feels there's a little something missing in your life?
- Do you have ambitions for a finer, richer life and aren't afraid to acknowledge them?
- Would you welcome the chance to put some impossible dreams into action and risk the consequences?
- Do you enjoy being with men, love their company, enjoy good sex, and want to enrich your sex life?
- Do you believe you're entitled to the best life has to

offer: a rewarding job, a loving man, a fulfilling family life?

- Are you willing to commit your energy and spirit to bettering your lot in life?
- Are you willing to take the responsibility for your own life, meeting life's twists and turns, triumphs and failures, and not blame luck, fate, or "enemies?"
- Are you ready to admit that love grows and multiplies by sharing, so you want to give and get more?

If you answered yes to most or all of these questions, then we have a lot in common. Like me, you cherish a few impossible dreams and secretly long to spread your wings just a little farther than they stretch now. You know it's risky, even dangerous. You're afraid of being hurt—who isn't?—but if someone gave you a push, you'd try. Well, Micki will push!

Twenty-five years ago, I first felt those same currents of ambition in me, and if I could feel them in the repressed 1950s, trussed up in a panty girdle, waist cincher, and push-up bra, you should be bowled over by them today!

Now, it's important to recognize one thing before we start this journey: Everything you want in life is out there waiting for you if you know how to get it and are willing to make the effort. I metamorphosed from an introverted Southern belle into an outgoing, aggressive actress and TV personality. Leaving a floundering marriage, I let go of the Prince Charming myth once and for all and learned to take care of myself. In my travels and profession, I met people from all walks of life. I threw out society's rule book and wrote my own. I created work for myself, I made money, I made opportunities. I took charge of my life. Actually, I made myself who I am today.

I challenged life and made some of my dreams come true. Better yet, they are still coming true, because I haven't stopped dreaming, striving—and getting.

Well, now you're up and revving on the path to success, have you thought about what it is?

I mean, does this big Success, capital everything, mean you'll be spending evenings draped in silk and spooning caviar out of Paul Newman's navel?

Not likely! Because that is only one image of success. It is not necessary to have your name in lights, a million dollars in the bank, or international acclaim to say you have a successful life. But if these are what you want, then go for them.

I know men and women whom the world sees as successful—big job, big house, big bank account, big show—but whom I would call losers. They've had a string of unhappy relationships, and they take a little pill every night to shut out the painful memories that keep popping into their heads. Is that Success? Not for this lady. Don't confuse success with having things piled on things. Maybe this ironic quote says it best: "Whoever has the most when he dies, wins!"

Success is getting what you want and admire and what pleasures you, but it's also enjoying all of it. It's being happy, not just with the people and possessions in your life, but with yourself.

Anybody can be a success if they know what success means to them. If deep in your heart you know there will be no happiness in your life until you open that art gallery, buy that condominium overlooking the bay, start a design company, or meet that man with a jet the color of your eyes, then that's what you have to pursue. Everyone's picture of success has a different personal coloring. A blanket goal of "success" covers nothing. Even though you may want more, parts of your life are probably already brimming with success.

People often ask me: Micki, do you consider yourself a success? And I tell them yes. Hah, they shoot back at me, then why haven't you made a movie with Robert Redford? Well, that's their measure of success, not mine. (Although I'm not saying no, Bob!)

I consider myself a successful person. I am proud of what I have achieved in my career, and I have an armful of successful relationships with a loving man, great children, and wonderful friends.

More important, I have a successful relationship with myself. I feel I have fulfilled my early promise and have more to accomplish. To me the biggest success is being able to live with myself, to sleep peacefully at night, liking who and what I am.

This doesn't mean that I have been smothered in success like a sundae in chocolate syrup.

I'm not going to tell you about the time I had one line in a commercial—"Mm,mm,good"—and it took seventy-two takes to get it right. I won't even mention the time I had my matinee idol and all-time heart throb Stewart Granger on the show. I had spent hours in makeup and was rushing to the studio when I tripped and fell headlong down a flight of stairs. I staggered into the studio with hair awry, pantyhose ripped, bruised, and bleeding from both kneecaps! My idol turned his matinee eyes on me and barked, "What the hell have you been doing, scrubbing floors?"

Let's not talk about the time I had to fly in a two-seater airplane for a TV commercial and sicked up all over my designer overalls or the time I posed with a live turkey under my arm to sell soap. If I told you all that you'd be discouraged and stop reading right now.

But with self-esteem and the inner knowledge of your true self, you can take all those ghastly mistakes with a grain (or bucket) of salt. Somewhere beneath layers of conditioning, presumptions, assumptions, and sidetracking, there is an elusive inner you waiting to astonish the world. It's that special talent and individuality that makes you different from your best friend, your worst enemy, your closest relation.

It is also the quirkiness that inspires people like me to sit on the chesterfield wearing a false nose and mustache, saying nothing, calmly reading the paper, when

Lisa brings home a new boyfriend, just to test his sense of humor, or to borrow and deliver a real live baby with a "Dear Poopsie, our little treasure is yours for the weekend" note to a corporate wizard for a birthday giggle. (Don't worry. I returned the baby.) It's all these little extras that make us us!

Now here is one of the most important things I can share with you: The journey to success depends on you. No one can carry you, no one can magically transport you to your goal. Only through hard work and desire will you reach it. Nobody gave me the right voice, the right amount of nerve, the qualifications. I had to work for them. Looking back I see my hand at work in all my successes, and that gives me more pleasure.

I had a girlfriend at university who had her life plan all mapped out. She was going to work in a different city each year, "to see what happened." If "nothing happened" (by which she meant no man, no fortune, no fame), she'd move on. At the end of ten years she'd given up looking, because obviously it wasn't out there. She was right about one thing: It isn't out there; it's in here. Outside factors will influence you, shape and mold you, intrigue, annoy, and fascinate you, color your thoughts and dreams, but your spirit, your basic hunger for life, is within. Your happiness is in your hands.

Let's stop here for a brief review:

- We've decided that you are ambitious for success, love, and all the other rewards of life.
- We've decided that your success will be uniquely tailored to your personality, needs, desires, and aptitudes.
- We've decided that only you can achieve your success, because no one else knows you and your abilities so well.

So what do we work on first?

Too much time is spent propping up the outside structure known as Me, Myself, and I and ignoring the inner needs. Those secret dreams, wishes, and ambitions have to be nourished.

Having said that, you'll probably come back at me with a dozen stories of women who walked out the door to fame, love, success, and a charmed life. My mother's favorite story was how Lana Turner was discovered sitting on a stool in Schwab's Drugstore and became an overnight star! If you sit around long enough looking gorgeous, someone (a producer, a husband, a millionaire) will find you and transform your life! Like most women of my generation, I believed in this "magic-think." It was easy; it took no effort. The only trouble was it didn't work.

It's amazing how early influences stay with you. I always have all my makeup on and my hair done, even just schlepping around at home. It's my "Darryl Zanuck" theory. When the megaproducer's car breaks down in front of my house, I'm ready! The only time I broke this rule was when I had to put the garbage out at the last minute. I staggered down to the end of the drive in my housecoat with no makeup on, my hair in rollers, and met my new neighbor for the first time. He introduced himself—a television producer! Oy, Mother!

If magic-think doesn't work, what does?

During my six years as a television host, I interviewed hundreds of people about their success in business, in sports, in love, and in their careers, and it always came down to the same rock-bottom line: belief in yourself. Nathaniel Branden, best-selling author and psychologist, defines self-esteem as a sense of personal worth, a combination of confidence and self-respect. People with self-esteem expect others to like them and respond warmly to them, because they like themselves. They have a special kind of confidence and contentment that shines from the inside out.

I can still see my cheeky five-year-old daughter the day she ran up to me and asked, "Know who I love best in the whole world, Mommy?"

"No," I replied coyly, puffing myself up to receive the Mother-of-the-Year award. "Who?"

"Myself!" She laughed happily and ran off!

After I'd pulled the dagger out of my heart, I couldn't help but be delighted. One of the first and most important building blocks—love of self—was firmly in place, and my little monster was on her way.

Nathaniel Branden told me that the first love affair we must consummate is with ourselves. I believe it. And that old adage that you have to love yourself before you can love another is also true. Self-love readies us for other relationships. This isn't vanity: It's self-discovery.

I grew up with a mixed bag of messages. One of them was to marry an ambitious man. Fair enough, but what about *my* ambitions? What was to happen to my dreams when I married? Was I supposed to have them cleaned and stored away like my wedding gown? At nineteen I had my BA and my MRS. Time to retire!

But under this sweet exterior there were the rumblings of an assertive woman. I knew I was intelligent, and I was willing to work hard for the things I wanted from life. So I worked and in so doing grew and changed.

For example, how did I know I could interview on television? I was working part-time as a student in a local Ohio station. The "real" reporters were all busy, so a harrassed editor sent me out. I hardly knew which end of the camera to speak to—I was a nervous, burbling bobby-soxer with a ponytail! But I discovered a great trick: If I asked a simple question and kept nodding my well-groomed head and saying uh-huh, uh-huh, people loved it. It gave them a chance no other reporter gave them—to talk uninterrupted! I also learned something else: I wasn't scared anymore.

Self-esteem and confidence are built through experience, through the choices you make of friends, lovers, careers, and interests. Knowing what you want as distinct from what society tells you to want makes the difference.

A healthy self-esteem, a solid inside structure, will serve as a powerful radar system in the decisions you make that direct your life.

• *Treat Yourself with Kid Gloves*

Don't you have days when you just want to die of exhaustion? Your job is running you ragged, your husband's running around, the kids are running through the house, and you're running in circles! Things are so ghastly, why not pile on a few more pressures and see if you can make the whole mess explode!

Know how good a professional massage feels after a muscle-ripping workout? Well, you need a kind of emotional massage and mental soother when the world gets rough, too.

I call it treating yourself with kid gloves.

When my kids were growing up I had to care for them, cook for a family, run the house, build my career, and tend to a dozen chores that seemed to fall on me from outer space. (Honestly, I don't know where else they'd come from. Who could have decided that I was the one to organize a Halloween costume sew-in?) I have vivid recollections of dropping into bed at the end of a day like a stone.

Today I treat myself better. I still have projects simmering, family commitments to fulfill, and wonderful Leonard to enjoy, but I always leave room to unwind, time to think, be with myself, and put problems aside. It's like a velvety fingertip massage for my soul.

Be good to yourself; there are enough well-meaning friends and relations out there who, intentionally or not, will trip you up and clutter your path. You don't have to be one of them. There's the husband who brings you chocolates just as you're starting your diet; the friend who relates ten medical horror stories when you take up jogging; the colleague who can't resist mentioning how many super-qualified people have applied for the job just before your interview.

At those times pull out those kid gloves!

Don't agonize over the jobs you didn't get; concentrate on the one you got.

Don't destroy yourself over the man who walked out; congratulate yourself on the one who stayed.

Don't dwell on the assignments you bungled; relive the ones you got right.

I learned the hard way. (Believe me, I have collected a lot of bruises!)

For years I'd had my eye on the TV, trying to figure out how I could get the rest of me on it. I watched commercials religiously. Here were people with people problems: bad breath, underarm odor, dripping noses, dirty laundry, pounding heads.

"Hey," I said to myself, "I've got all those things."

Then one morning my sink stopped up. It was an omen. I looked in the mirror and said, "I am a real person with a real person's problem."

Did I call a plumber? Of course not; I called an agent. Getting the agent was easy; getting a job was not.

When I began auditioning for television commercials, the calls were for "modern young housewives." Out I sailed, made up as mother taught me and dressed for discovery—and continually unemployed.

Finally I ambushed my agent and asked why.

Her reply astounded me. She cast her eye over my hair, dress, and makeup and said, "Honey, you don't look like a housewife."

"But I am," I wailed. "I'm a wife, I have a house, I've got two kids and a budgie."

Did I quit? Did I give up? No! I went shopping. I bought a sensible shirtwaist dress, a pair of semi-orthopedic shoes, and a short, mousey-brown wig. In this disguise, I wowed the producers who "knew" a housewife when they saw one! And I got the job! And the next one and the one after that. I looked like a lady who

11

knew how to handle ring around the collar.

These are the successes I remember—the one, two, three, thirty successes—not the hundred and fifty ego-bruising rejections.

Another part of treating yourself right is being honest about your abilities and setting realistic goals. There's no point yearning for a pilot's license if you're deathly afraid of heights or breaking your heart to be a fashion model if you're five foot zero.

Take it from me. Like every girl who dreams of becoming an actress, I had prepared my acceptance speech for the Academy Awards before I was out of my teens! Somewhere along the way—I think after making a horror film called *Necromania* (okay, okay, so it didn't have great social and political significance; but it did have a catchy slogan: "The Wages of Sin are Syphillis, Gonorrhea, and Death")—I realized little Oscar would never be mine. Katherine Hepburn had nothing to fear from Micki Moore!

Did I quit? No! I just set a more realistic goal. Another movie (any other movie), some television spots (any TV spot—okay, okay, I'll be the chicken!), more commercials, and one day, maybe, my own television show. Grab that grease pencil! Hello, Success!

One of the secrets of treating yourself right is not setting yourself up for failure.

We all know instant enthusiasts who take up jogging with the determination of a bulldog and try to go ten miles the first morning. Or begin that new diet bent on losing twenty pounds the first week. Or how about the graduate who must become company president in a year. They'll never make it! Superman couldn't make it! A big part of succeeding is being realistic. It's easier to keep going on small successes than large failures.

Pat is the perfect example of this. When her twins were toddlers she sold cosmetics in her spare (!) time. She figured if she really hustled she could sell $1000 worth of face paint a week. In two weeks she had a cheque for $40, owed the sitter $50, and was dejected.

"I guess I'm not a businesswoman, Micki," she sighed.

"Well, not a multinational conglomerate, anyway," I consoled her. "Door-to-door cosmetic sales depend on people contacts. Forget about the money for the time being and try to make four new contacts a week."

Pat was like a starving terrier with a bone! Off she roared, armed with her new approach. She saw four new women the first week, four the second, five the third, and before she knew it she had a clientele and a profitable business. Pat's luck didn't change, just her perspective. She tackled the same project with a realistic goal, one over which she had some control. She set herself up for success and came up a winner.

Many of the successful people I've interviewed have made painful mistakes. But they had the ability to get up quickly after a fall, dust themselves off, and try again. Rarely did they make the same mistake twice; neither will you. Believe me, there is an imprint in the sidewalk somewhere for all the times I've fallen on my face.

Not winning is *not* failure.

It is a stepping stone, a maturing process that teaches you something about yourself and the way of the world. View it as a dress rehearsal—for the next time.

It also helps if you hook up with others who treat themselves with kid gloves. Life, as you may have noticed, is a constant battle between Yes- and No-people.

Yes, try that. You might discover some hidden talent.

No, you can't possibly be an artist. You'll starve.

Yes, you should take the chance, even if you have to live in a shoebox!

No, don't be a fool. Security is the most important thing in life.

Yes, I believe things will get better.

No, things could get worse. Be careful, don't rock the boat.

I love the Yes-people: Their openness, optimism, and

willingness to take chances inspire me. No-people I avoid. They work so hard at discouraging you, spreading their doom and gloom. But as somebody (obviously a Yes-person) once said, "Great spirits always encounter opposition from mediocre minds."

I've even made some converts to this point of view.

There was a talented but No-ish woman working with me at the television network. We were both in Variety, but she longed to be in the newsroom and was insane with ambition when an opening came up.

"Micki, I won't get the job," she said gloomily one day over lunch. "The others applying have all got loads of experience and are better qualified. They won't hire me."

"I don't blame them," I said. "After listening to you, I wouldn't hire you, either. Never mind what they can do—concentrate on what *you* can do," I told her. "You've done research, you've assisted in directing, you've done production work. Tell them that. The rest you can learn."

Now when I see her name roll up on the credits of a major national newscast, I tell myself: There goes another Yes-person, formerly a No-person, straight to the top.

• Finding the Missing Pieces

I was accused of being a cold-hearted bitch the same day an acquaintance threw her arms around me in the middle of traffic and declared I was "all heart." I come home bristling with energy after what I think is a pretty aggressive show on my part in contract negotiations, and Leonard laughs at my puffball tactics.

So which is it? And which is it with you? I once took an acting class in which we analyzed our characters in terms of head, heart, or gut and how each would react to the world.

Head people are thinkers, operating from logic, reason, and rules.

Heart people are all feelings. They are emotional escalators, always way up in exultation or way down in crisis.

Gut people are the risk-takers; they leap first, look later. They don't wait for the world to find them; they take it by storm.

Each of us, of course, is made up of all three parts, but one usually leads. To function fully and effectively you have to work at bringing all three pieces together, integrating and developing them into an intuitive system of checks and balances. It's part of that strong foundation we've been talking about. You need to be in touch with each part—how can you communicate and share your thoughts and feelings with others if you don't understand them yourself?

I work at keeping the pieces trotting along in harmony, although every once in a while one of them gallops ahead. It's usually my gut, and off I leap into a blind risk. Sometimes it pays off, sometimes not—like the time I turned down a movie part to do what I thought was a major network documentary on a revolutionary new operating theater technique. It turned out to be about a dog having a tonsillectomy!

However, there was also the time I decided Canada needed an exercise show. This was twenty years ago, when Jane Fonda was still posing for cheesecake posters and "workout" was something trainers gave racehorses. The sensible (head) thing to do was write a detailed professional letter to station management outlining my qualifications.

Not me! I just phoned up, asked to speak to a producer, any producer, and told him Canadians needed to touch their toes. Three days later I was on the air, with leotard, tights, and an almost nonexistent knowledge of exercise. (But I learned fast: I'll never be a No-person.) It was reckless, silly, impulsive—and wildly successful. Sometimes impulses are wings.

But I couldn't possibly live that way. Not all the time. A friend of mine, licking her wounds from yet another doomed love affair, complained: "I still can't understand what happened. It was electric and passionate for about a month, then boom! He left with the same conviction he stayed. He decided to go back to his wife."

Listening to her story, I realized that the characters had changed, but the plot was the same as in each of her last three involvements. "Why don't you control the speed of the relationship?" I asked. "Why don't you take more time to get to know the man before investing yourself so heavily?"

"That's just not possible," she said. "I always follow my heart."

"Why don't you follow your head for once?" I replied.

"I can't. That's just the way I am."

Unwilling to believe that she had any choice in the matter, she continually set herself up for a letdown. The truth, however, is that for her—and for you—there are always choices.

"Choice," says Dr. Harvey Silver, a frequent guest on "You're Beautiful," "is the most important word in the English language." If you believe you're capable of choosing to think and feel certain things, things that make you happy, then you can stop making choices that make you unhappy. "If I want to change how I feel," continues Dr. Silver, "I have to change how I think."

Do this simple exercise: Close your eyes, think, visualize a car hitting your closest friend or your child. In a matter of seconds, your face will cringe, you'll feel anguish through your body. Now visualize yourself lying on a sunny beach holding hands with the person you love, listening to the surf. Your face will relax, your whole body will smile, you'll feel warm and wonderful. It's what you bring to a situation that determines what you do with it.

If you think it's natural to be depressed and angry, if you believe personalities can't change without years of analysis, if you're sure that all your problems stem from an unhappy childhood or that you're just "that kind of person" (head, heart, or gut) and nothing can change that, then nothing will.

But why do we choose to be unhappy?

When my marriage of thirteen years ended, it took me a long time to recover from the impact of shattered dreams and failed expectations. Why did this happen, what did we do wrong? Everyone must go through this cleansing process, but I dwelt on my pain long past the normal mourning period. Finally a good friend asked me point blank: "Why are you choosing to hang onto the pain?"

I was shocked. I hadn't realized I'd been clutching it so tightly for so long. So pulling head, heart, and gut together and drawing on every ounce of self-esteem that I had left, I let the pain go.

"I don't have to be miserable," I told myself (I talk to myself a lot), I don't have to feel badly, I can let go and be happy."

It's important for each of us to find and develop our missing pieces so that our head, heart, and gut start to work in tandem. It's part of the growing process; it's part of getting stronger; it's part of being everything you can be.

• *Stumbling Blocks—Clearing the Path*

One day I realized I had to learn to talk.

On camera.

On paper this sounds obvious, but you should have heard the Micki Moore of old, drawling out the syllables in her high-pitched, creamy-thick Southern accent. Two years of sweating at elocution lessons finally turned "Hayoou Nayoou Brraaoun Cayoau" into "How Now Brown Cow."

My voice was the biggest stumbling block to my career. But at least it was a recognizable one. Other stumbling blocks that hold women back or bind them in unhappy situations are hidden. They prevent women from reaching their full potential and force them to act

17

in ways which in their hearts they know are wrong.

Toni suffers this way.

"I want to go away for the weekend with my new boyfriend, but my father won't let me," she confided one day over coffee.

I was stunned. This was no challenging teenager talking, but a woman in her late forties who'd been divorced for seven years!

"What do you mean he won't let you?" I demanded.

Slowly she answered, "I asked him what he thought of Bill and I going away for the weekend, and he gave me that look. He doesn't approve, so I can't go."

"But do you approve?" I asked cautiously.

Yes, she said, but she wouldn't upset Daddy.

Poor Toni. Poor Daddy. Poor Bill.

Although an independent woman in many ways, Toni still seeks parental permission and approval before she acts. Toni's hooked on that soothing drug: approval. As children we need it so badly that it's hard to kick the habit. Forsaking the need for approval from others is forsaking the security of childhood. The idea is terrifying. But it's necessary if we're going to grow up and accept the responsibility of our own choices and decisions.

It matters to us that people we love think well of us, and that's good. But when it comes to the crunch and it's time to act, the only approval we need is our own. Disapproval is hard to stand up to, but if you don't you'll never really stand on your own two feet.

Gently I've tried to wean my own children from the approval habit.

Lisa called long distance and frantic in the middle of the afternoon from her university: "Mother, help! I'm changing courses, and I want your approval."

"Lisa, darling," I told her. "You are eighteen years old, and you don't need my approval. What you want and what I'll give you is my opinion. You can agree or disagree, but you must make your own decision."

When young birds leave the nest, they have to fly solo!

How many other stumbling blocks are in the way of getting what you want?

The Compassion Trap   "Wonderful" is how Eileen's friends and family describe her. They lean on her for support, they cry on her shoulder, she mops up their tears and gives them all the comfort, reassurance, and compassion they need. To them she's the Red Cross, Salvation Army, and Santa Claus all rolled into one.

To me it's excessive—wasteful of her emotional strength, spirit, and sensitivity. Like a bank account where it's all pay-out and no pay-in, she's just about empty.

Love is not a one-way street. Of course you love your family, and of course they come to you with their problems. I've lost count of the number of broken hearts, outrages, and full-scale wars I've smoothed over with two kids growing up under my roof. I listened, I comforted, I helped them sort things out—but after all the discussion and tears, I handed their problems back to them for resolution.

Too many women lug around everyone's emotional baggage and can't remember what it's like not to feel overburdened. You can offer advice, opinions, and support—but having done that, offer the problem back to the person whose problem it really is. You've got problems of your own to attend to.

Worry and Fear   "Worry is like a rocking chair," said someone who knew. "It gives you something to do, but it doesn't get you anywhere." Worrying is a surefire way to feel helpless and defeated.

To quote from Dr. Silver again, "Feeling worried or guilty or anxious is an escape mechanism against dealing effectively with the present moment. The only moment you can live in is the present one. All past moments are gone forever, and the future is just going to be another present moment. Next time you're worried, ask yourself: "What might I be doing instead? Then start doing it."

No matter how many speeches I give to women's groups, fundraisings, and business organizations, I'm always a wreck before I hit the podium. I used to sit and chew the tablecloth, but now I take action. I sit in the audience for a while, chatting in great over-the-fence style, and by speech time I've warmed up, I've met some people I like, and there's been no time to worry.

Dr. Silver is right: *Action defeats fear*!

Criticism   After swimming eighty laps, I hauled myself out of the pool looking like a cross between a drowned rat and a shriveled prune. I heard two sunbathers say, "See, she looks so much better on TV."

Is there anybody out there who isn't vulnerable to criticism? Criticism is part of life, and there's no escape (after all, sometimes we deserve it). It hurts most when it comes from people closest to you: people you love and trust not to hurt you. When your kid brother tells you that you look like Miss Piggy in a bikini, you can aim a punch at him and forget it, but when a new lover tells you the same thing . . .

The friend who tells you that your presentation to the board was awful, who points out how your voice shook and how you called the client Mr. Dumbbell instead of Mr. Beldum, is taking the day off from being your friend, I'd say.

Okay, everyone knows there are two kinds of criticism.

There's the constructive kind that might actually help you change something that, deep down, you want to change, like procrastinating at work or a negative attitude. Always be ready to learn from someone who is genuinely interested in your betterment.

Then there's the destructive kind that's not aimed at fixing anything but at putting the fix on you. It hurts, it's often unjust (but with a big enough element of truth to make it sting), and it doesn't do you any good to hear it.

One thing I've learned: Separate what you do from who you are. A lot of carping criticizers get you on this one. Just because you botched one job or one assignment does not mean you are permanently impaired, stupid, ineffective, or ready for the trash pile. Okay, you make a mistake. Next assignment, please.

Someone once said that if you give a woman a compliment she'll question it. Insult her and she won't. Don't go looking for criticism. Believe me, there's enough around, and some of it will stick.

Fear of criticism can be paralyzing. One talented friend creates exquisite canvasses that decorate her basement. When I insist she should have a show, she replies, "I'm not sure my paintings are good enough. Maybe no one will like them, and I couldn't bear the critics' negative comments." Yet in her heart of hearts she wishes to be recognized for the talent that I can assure you, and her, she has. It's not the critics blocking her path: It's her fear of criticism.

Perfectionism I was born with a streak of it. I'm sure I arranged the blankets in my crib until they were just so. I have driven Leonard berserk fiddling with a flower arrangement, moving purple, yellow, white, pink around for best effect.

High standards and goals are good for us. They stretch our potential to the limit. They make us dream and pursue excellence. But there is a fine line between the pursuit of excellence and perfectionism. The perfectionist must always do everything right; there is no room for error. If this is you, pin this up on your bulletin board:

21

"Aim for excellence and you'll get to be top banana;
Aim for perfection and you'll go bananas." (courtesy
Lynn Tribbling)

Standards have to be reachable if we're going to enjoy the upward climb. The purpose of all this striving
and trying and growing is to enjoy life more, or have
you forgotten?

Perfectionists magnify their mistakes a thousand
times. ("Leonard, I knew I should have put the pink
tulips in front, not behind the daffodils." "Micki, will
you please stop sobbing on the couch and come to
bed.") They can't understand why the whole world
isn't in shock. The truth is, the whole world doesn't
care. It's got problems of its own. Always, always do
and be the best you can—and forget the rest.

• Why Do I Look in the Mirror and See Only My Faults?

By the tender age of eleven I was already five foot
seven inches tall. I didn't have to look far (or high) to
find a fault! But how could I worry about my height
when there were more desperate things to worry about?
Like my nose.

In the movie magazines I devoured as a teenager, I
unearthed a vital gem of information: Elizabeth Taylor
wore a clothespin on her nose at night to "turn it up."

Immediately I clipped on a clothespin.

Then I discovered my ears and so, I figured, had the
rest of the world, they stuck out so far. I taped them flat
against my head.

Somehow I survived these afflictions and grew up to
learn that individual beauty is just that—individual. Our
differences are what we should celebrate.

What do you think of when I mention Barbra Strei-
sand? Isn't it that soaring voice and quirky personality?
Or Bette Midler? Madcap energy and outrageousness.
Or actress Karen Black? Sexiness and sensuality.

But by conventional standards Streisand is an ugly

duckling, Bette's nose is too big, and Karen's eyes are too close together. Does anyone care? All three women (and thousands of others) have defied conventional beauty standards to create their own beauty. They have made the mind-body connection. They think beautiful, therefore they are.

Part of that beauty is self-assurance. No matter how "odd" they look, no matter how "different" different is, they believe themselves compelling.

It's not the way you look but the way you feel about how you look. I interviewed hundreds of women on my TV show—everyone from exotic beauties such as Diane von Furstenberg to feisty personalities like Billie Jean King to housewives, career women, and psychologists—real people with real stories. It was fascinating to see what kind of magic the camera picked up. People who were magazine-cover attractive sometimes didn't come across very well, and many who didn't fit society's beauty standards would shine. You couldn't take your eyes off them. They knew their information, and they spoke with such authority, concern, and understanding. What disappeared was the external, and what appeared was what I call the overall image of a person, their presence. I think that's what matters, that's what counts.

Actress June Wilkinson, who runs a successful exercise studio, told me that not one woman who walks through her door is satisfied with the way she looks. From chubby housewife to anorexic model, they all sigh and cry over their imperfect bodies. These arms are too flabby, these thighs too lumpy, this tummy too fat. Why is what we have never good enough?

Do men do this so devoutly? Of course not. Why do bright, attractive, successful women weep in front of a full-length mirror? Part of it is knowing we can never measure up to the gorgeous airbrushed images pushed at us by advertisers and fashion arbitrators. But no amount of diet, exercise, and prayer will turn the body of a Russian shot-putter into one of racehorse-thin elegance. There is only one way to come to terms with

this: Get yourself into the best shape possible, whatever that is, and stop pining for Farrah's legs or Joan
Collins's bustline. Take my son's advice about the beat-
up old Volkswagen he was driving when his cronies all
had sports cars: Just fix it up and learn to love it!

• No One Can Take Away What Is Yours

Okay, so up till now you've done everything right.
You've worked hard and put in the time and effort and
sacrificed and achieved, and your big chance has finally landed in your lap.

Then Malignant Fate swipes it away!

After four years of playing fan bearers, letter carriers,
and spear handlers, you're finally given a speaking
role—and are struck down with laryngitis.

After slaving away in penury at law school, you're
hired by the firm of your dreams—and it goes bank-
rupt.

After loving your man through his toughest career
years, supporting him, ironing his shirts, and suffering
his tantrums, he gets the president's office—and runs
off with the president's secretary.

It happens. It's easy to feel you've lost everything. All
you've striven for, anguished over, learned, and are
eager to put to use is worthless. Even worse, you feel
you're worthless, too.

Let me tell you about Alexis.

Every moment she could spare away from her rent-
paying job in an insurance company was devoted to
breaking into film production. She took night courses
and workshops and volunteered endlessly for documentary work. Then her night school teacher offered
her a job on a film he was editing for a New York
production house. Alexis closed the typewriter cover
and settled into a year of twenty-hour days, roughing it
on location, and being part of an award-winning team.
She was ecstatic.

"Micki, I am living my dreams," she said.

No sooner had she spoken than the dream was shattered.

She and her producer-mentor had a fiery falling out. He packed up and went off to California, and Alexis went off the deep end.

"That's it," she sobbed. "It's the end of my dreams. I love this work, and it's gone."

"Instead of mourning what you've lost, why don't you use what you've gained?" I asked her. She looked puzzled, so I explained: "All the contacts you've made, the skills you've learned, and the initiative you have—they're all still yours. Find another producer. Make your own film."

One contact led to another: a little job here, a bigger job there, an ounce of recognition, a pound of fame . . . Today Alexis is in film production in a big way—New York, L.A., Cannes. At last she believes her skills are part of *her*, not just part of her current project.

The lesson, desperadoes, is that what is yours . . . is yours. Nobody can steal it from you any more than they can steal your soul. It's a lesson that takes a long time to understand, longer still to believe. Until that time, here's a survival kit to help you on the journey.

II

Micki Moore's Survival Kit

Haven't you noticed that when one part of your life falls apart—your job, your relationship, your best friendship—everything else falls with it?

Your boss dumps on you for missing a contract, your man picks this moment to leave town, your friend decides she can live without you—and suddenly you're alone.

Yes, there are times when life seems too tough and too unfair to keep going. There are no fair-trade laws in love or work, and there's no one you can sue. One thing slips out of place and, like dominoes, your whole life comes tumbling down (or it feels like it). What can you do but run in circles on negative energy!

I've been caught in this whirlpool of gloom and doubt enough times to know. But just when I feel I'm going under for the third time, I reach for my Survival Kit. I'd like to report it contains a magnum of champagne and a beautiful new man, but it's more lasting than that: It's a combination of everything I've learned, often painfully, about building bridges over gulfs of failure. These are the wings that pick up a sinking spirit and remind me I'm still the same person who just a few weeks ago was succeeding on all fronts.

There have been times when emotional and financial trauma have threatened to overwhelm and I've thought I just can't go on another day. But I've survived by telling myself that *one event does not a lifetime make*.

27

It sounds loopy, but Little Orphan Annie was right—the sun really does come up tomorrow!

Okay, so the basement is so full of water that a family of ducks has moved in, and okay, so the man I thought of marrying has run off with the housekeeper, and now I don't have a housekeeper to change the sheets or a man to sleep on them. Okay, so my agent just offered me the part of a grandmother on the eve of my fortieth birthday, when I've been telling myself all day that life begins at forty! So, okay! As miserable as this domestic disaster, unhappy love affair, and job change make me, the misery won't hold me in gloomy thrall forever. There is real pain and suffering in our lives that needs to be acknowledged. Mourn, bury it, and get on with living.

But it's crazy to think you can get through tough times unprepared and empty-handed. Would you go into a boxing ring without gloves?

As much as the spirit to fight back, you need the equipment. It will take time and struggle to gather the pieces together for yourself. But my personal survival kit will teach you how to land on your feet anyplace, anytime, with anyone.

• Humor Heals

Without a sense of humor I would have curled up in a ball and died long ago! From embarrassment, mainly! Humor has let me live through life's ridiculous, awkward, provoking, hopeless moments with a smidgen of grace and self-esteem intact.

To me laughter is as necessary as oxygen. It's a buoy that keeps us afloat when all else is sinking. It's the glue, the putty that holds us together in a world that's falling apart. It's the playful, reckless child in us releasing worry and depression. Laughter puts the perspective into life. Awful things happen out there, and you can either laugh or cry over them—I prefer to laugh.

You don't need to wait for something to be uproariously funny before you laugh. Humor is much more than joking, and there's a trace of it in everything from first dates to funerals.

It is the great defense mechanism. If I'm in a situation that makes me uncomfortable or tense, I usually laugh. I've used laughter to help others, too. Before the taping of a television show, the poor guests are herded into a pre-interview room where the tension builds like a storm cloud. Laughter has cut through that tension like a silver knife.

Before each show, I'd drop in to see the guests to try and put them at ease. If they were unaccustomed to being interviewed or to being under the lights of a television studio, I could spot TV terror in their eyes from twenty feet.

Then I discovered how a few jokes or wisecracks could loosen them up. "You can do anything you like on camera, but don't pick your nose," I'd tell them, and a few thin smiles would emerge. If I could get them to laugh just a little before that camera blinked on, not only would their bodies relax, but their minds would also unfold with relief. They'd transform into wonderfully responsive and open talkers.

Occasionally it worked the other way around—a guest would be too at home in the limelight, and I would be the one who had to be rescued.

Gay Talese, who wrote the inside story of the sexual revolution in *Thy Neighbor's Wife* after years of living in communes and prowling around massage parlors and red light districts, was one of those.

Our interview was going fine until the first commercial break. As we "went to black," Talese leaned over and whispered, "You are very beautiful, and I wanna f--- you."

Did I faint? Did I scream? (Remember, this is only a sixty-second break.)

No. I calmly called over the director and asked her,

"Do you think we could stop the production for half an hour or so?" "Are you crazy?" she said. "We're going live to tape," and stomped away.

"Sorry, Mr. Talese," I said. "No time. The show must go on."

And on we went with neither of us blushing!

Laughter can stop the most unpromising situations from turning nasty. For example, when we went through contract negotiations at the station (a hideous time for everybody), all the good humor and camaraderie normally in the air melted away.

Returning from the studio to the dressing room during one of these times, I passed the station manager in his office, toiling over his books and probably figuring out how he could get away with not paying me. I was dressed, I should add, in full gypsy regalia, left over from the taping of a fantasy fashion show. I spun into his office with a bloodcurdling yell and leaped onto his desk, stamping my bare feet all over his budget, banging the tambourine, and waving my red and black skirts about while he backed into the wall in terror.

"Give her anything she wants," he gasped to his astonished secretary. "Just get her out of here."

We were all laughing, and the tension and animosity building between us disappeared.

I've known humor to work on the job, at dinner parties, on first dates—anywhere people are trying hard to be comfortable but are floundering. Laughter is a positive, zestful reaction to life and one that's hard for anyone to turn away from.

Can anything that makes you feel this good be good for you?

Believe it or not, mounting medical evidence indicates that laughter gives almost every organ in the body a healthy workout! It turns on the adrenalin, tenses the diaphragm and abdominal muscles, quickens the heart rate, and increases lung pressure. Honest!

If you laugh so much you hurt, your pituitary gland (this is getting so medical) releases endorphins, the body's natural painkillers. After a good laugh, don't you feel relaxed and pleasured? It proves beyond a doubt that laughter is the best medicine.

Now stop laughing and listen: Laughter transforms the unpleasant, the painful, the hurtful into something you can face and cope with. It knocks the fear and worry out of problems and cuts them down to manageable size. Humor mixed with courage is an unbeatable combination.

One of my favorite stories of the heroic rescuing power of humor is about a young woman traveling on public transit who suddenly feels a male hand creeping across her bottom. In a booming voice she announces to every passenger on the bus, "Will whoever belongs to the hand on my ass PLEASE TAKE IT OFF!" Exit one mortified molester with applause for the wisecracking woman.

I was in a not unsimilar situation in, of all places, a hospital! A male fan jammed the revolving door so I couldn't escape and crooned, "Micki, you're beautiful. I won't let you out of this door until you promise to have a coffee with me."

What could I do? My friend upstairs could wait for her flowers and fruit; I had a nut to deal with first. We went to the hospital coffee shop (it was the least romantic place I could think of), and a sympathetic waitress let us sit at a table in the "This Section Closed" section. My admirer kept on the attack.

"Micki, I want to make love to you," he said.

"Well, that's nice," I replied, "but we'll have to do it over there; this section is closed," and I got up and left. I hope he tipped the waitress.

The recognition that goes along with celebrity has given me some laughs in the most unexpected places. Walking through the lobby of a luxurious downtown hotel, I heard a woman screaming at the top of her voice. I ran in the direction of the sound—the women's washroom. I flung open the door of a cubicle, and there, standing on the toilet seat wearing a fur coat and

31

clutching her pantyhose around her knees, was a terrified woman.

"What's the matter?" I asked.

"A man just stuck his head under the door ... he tried to grab my ankle and ..." (stunned pause) "Hey, aren't you Micki Moore?"

I assured her I was, that there was no man there any longer, and that it was safe to come out. We left laughing.

A sense of humor can shorten the distance between two strangers and open doors that "proper" behavior keeps closed forever.

When comedian Dudley Moore, whom I adore, was performing years ago in a stand-up comedy routine, I was tempted, like many other fans, to go backstage. Instead I sent him a note: "Dudley," it read, "I'm dying to meet you, but I have an urgent appointment with my gynecologist and can't stay after the show." I included my telephone number. Intrigued, Dudley called! Unfortunately he called from the airport on his way to the next tour stop, but the note had appealed instantly to his wacky sense of humor, and we established an immediate rapport. If he hadn't been flying out ... who knows?

Sometimes life hands you such a smack in the face that to survive at all you have to learn to laugh at yourself. It's usually the hardest joke to take, the one where you are the punch line. But I always remind myself of the quote: "An optimist laughs to forget; a pessimist forgets to laugh."

A testimonial here—the most wonderful things can blossom from the most unintentionally funny beginnings. While I was doing "You're Beautiful," I had a deal that my on-air wardrobe would be supplied by Anne Klein at no cost. Part of that deal, or so I thought, was a supply of coordinating shoes from Town Shoes, the company owned by Leonard.

At that time both Leonard and I were members of the same tennis club and nodded at each other over the net, although we'd never spoken. I was calling his company every couple of days about those damn shoes, and the company president kept putting me off. Finally I decided: What have I got to lose? A game of tennis at most, so I approached Leonard at the club. Sweetly I told him of my predicament, and sweetly he listened to every detail before telling me to call his president again in the morning. I could hardly wait to make that call, after all that president had put me through.

But when I did, he said, "No shoes." Leonard had said not to give them to me! What a sweetheart! I just figured, well, some you lose. But worse from Leonard was to come.

Six months later, he approached me over the net and said, "We're opening a new shoe store in town, and we need a celebrity to help open it." I glowed. "But," he continued, "if we can't get a real celebrity, will you come?"

How could I resist a man as endearing as that? Leonard and I now share a home, and our lives!

• Intuition

You've got it. Use it.

Why? Because it works.

When Englebert Humperdinck was guesting on "You're Beautiful," he predictably showed up with a block-long entourage of managers, publicity people, wardrobe "helpers," and enough gofers for the rajah of a small kingdom. They all had instructions for me.

"Miss Moore, under no circumstances can you ask him about his paternity suits." "Please refrain from mentioning any album that didn't go gold." "He won't answer questions about his early family life." "Mr. Humperdinck refuses to talk about comparisons with Tom Jones." And by the way, they added, he'll only stay fifteen minutes. He doesn't do half-hour shows.

Well, why don't we just shut down the studio and go home? I wondered.

But as I looked at Humperdinck, who had come into the studio barely able to move for the swarm of hangers-on around him, something just told me that if I got him away from his keepers, he would open up and chat until dawn.

The show's producer wasn't convinced. "If he walks out after fifteen minutes, we'll be left with half a show of empty tape," she said. "We'd better line someone up for the second half."

"No," I told her, "I have a feeling right here. My instincts tell me this one will be okay."

She backed off, not about to get into a debate about my "instincts."

And as usual they were right on target.

Once the cameras were rolling, Englebert was a charming, gracious talker, and he answered all my questions—including those in the "forbidden zones." He stayed for the full thirty minutes and looked almost disappointed when it was over and his managers stepped forward to claim him again.

Afterward the producer chided me: "It was close, Micki. If he'd decided to walk off we'd have lost a show."

How could I explain that my intuition—that unscientific, immeasurable marvel—had told me it would be okay and I believed it? That I trusted it, and it had never let me down since I learned to listen to it.

But what is it? Intuition is my sixth sense, my radar, my antennae advising me to move toward this person, away from that one.

Businessmen know it; it's that gut feeling that tells them to buy a thousand shares of hoola hoops. Lovers know it: It's that heart-flip across a crowded room that tells two strangers they will be lovers. It can be better than two college degrees, but you have to believe in it or it won't work.

For years I couldn't trust mine. It went against everything I'd been taught in school and out there in the "logical" world. Facts counted, not feelings. Yet often when the facts said "No," my feelings said "Yes," and finally I listened.

Now intuition is part of my "silent script," the real-life equivalent of an actor's silent script. It's the message written between the lines, the message picked up by the audience despite the words coming out of the characters' mouths. You know the kind of thing—two people say they love each other, but we all know she is having an affair and he is planning to run off with the upstairs maid. There's just as much silent scripting in real life if we could just learn to read it.

Often people who could read a friend's script in a blink of an eye are blind to their own. Susannah is like that. She turned up on my doorstep one morning (in the middle of Phil Donahue—almost unforgiveable!) half-raging, half-sobbing.

"He's left!" she stormed.

"Phil Donahue?" I asked, looking at the benign face on the television screen.

"No, no, no. Paul's left. Just left with no warning, no apology, no explanation, nothing. How could he?"

How could *she*, I wondered, be so blind to the distress signals flashing around their relationship for the last six months? Hadn't Susannah herself complained about his late nights at work and vague out-of-town assignments? Hadn't she bemoaned the fact that he refused to make future plans about buying a house, and hadn't she interrupted Donahue and me just a month before to complain how lousy her sex life had become?

Hadn't she said then that things didn't "feel right" between them? How much intuition, feelings, sensitivity can one woman ignore? If she'd read the writing on the wall earlier, maybe the wall wouldn't have come crashing down on top of her.

Susannah is one of those people who smother their intuitive feelings because they sometimes tell them things that are too painful to hear. But those delicate little antennae of intuition quivering in warning now can spare us a lot of pain in the future.

"But if something doesn't feel right, I always think I can fix it," Susannah says. "It's not like a for-sure fact of life . . ."

It is, Susannah, and all the hundreds out there like you.

An emotional fact of life is still a fact of life. Feelings guide you through dangerous waters in a way logic can't. Feelings take you into deeper, darker, more dangerous places, and we should listen to them carefully, thoughtfully, with all our hearts.

Time and time again it's worked for me, in a personal relationship and in professional ones.

Maureen McTeer arrived on my show with a list of no-no questions, particularly about Joe Clark and his brief, shining hour as PM. I could "feel" her protectiveness, her defensiveness, her resistance to opening up old wounds. But I also "felt" that if I treated her in the right way, she'd open up—and she did. She answered all the questions, including the difficult, unpleasant, and awkward ones, and she went home happy. I intuitively knew what was holding her back, and she responded with intuition of her own, feeling that here was an interviewer she could trust a little. Free-flowing intuition can be so productive.

No one likes to downgrade woman's intuition more than men. (Maybe because they've been victims of it once too often!) Yet some of the most powerful businessmen and politicians rely on it every day. They call it by another name, of course—hunch or flash or gut feeling—but they use it and are admired for it, because it works.

Now I know you're going to say, "Won't I become a dreamy, ineffectual person if I trust my feelings?"

The answer is no.

Tuning in to your feelings is not the same as being ruled by them. If it feels more comfortable, call it not ignoring them or not ruling them out.

I've been accused of being dreamy, and it's true that intuitive people are daydreamers. But I believe that understanding your daydreams can tell you a lot about what's missing in your life.

A businessman with a reputation for ruthlessness and coldness once confessed to me that he daydreamed constantly about romance—not sex—but romance, on a cruise ship, on a desert island, in a supermarket, in a rush-hour subway! He had recently been divorced and craved love and affection. I hope his dreams came true before too long.

Intuitive people are usually brimming with confidence. They can afford to be when they've got feelings as well as brains going for them. They're usually self-sufficient. You don't have to depend on the feelings of the world when you can trust your own. Depending on your own feelings sows a supreme confidence in yourself. Ask any successful (read intuitive) businessman whose "feelings" have just made him sell and buy shares at the right moment and fatten his bank account. Or any woman whose intuition has steered her away from the handsome stranger (sigh) at the dinner party who, when not making hot eyes at her, is admiring his reflection in the soup plate. Trouble there!

Despite all the evidence, logicians will crusade against intuition as if it were a disease.

Don't debate with them. Intuition defies explanation, so if you believe in it, you've got it. Develop it. See it as a strength. It carries you over the biggest hurdles in life when you can say, in addition to "I know it's true," "I feel it's true."

• Resourcefulness

What do you want to be when you grow up? I asked myself one morning when my agent had just offered me the umpteenth coffee commercial, a chance to sit in a rocking chair, and say "Ahhhhhhh" again as I sip.

I want, I answered myself, to have my own television show.

No problem, the conversation continued, but how to get it?

I wanted a TV talk show so badly that I decided the only way to get it was to give it to myself. So with some willing friends I made a demonstration tape. For more than a year, I hawked it around to every local station that would let me in the door.

"Hi again, honey," the producers would say as I made my rounds with the by now worn-out tape clutched to my bosom. Their response was always the same: Thanks for trying, and you have nice teeth!

But I refused to give up. And incredibly, one of the local stations, CITY, decided they needed an afternoon talk show. Guess who they remembered? The "crazy" (read resourceful) lady who walked around with her own show tucked under her arm. They called, I auditioned, and I got the job. (Talk about having a clear vision of what you want! How could I fail? I'd been living it for a year in my head.)

Resourcefulness won't always pay off so dramatically, but it will always pay off. If it proves only that you can meet the challenges and demands of life, it's a must-have quality. There are times (the majority) when you have to do for yourself what nobody is willing to do for you.

Resourcefulness is a great rarity. Those blessed with it, with this ability of never giving up until they've found a way around a problem, are blessed indeed. They are the winners who never say, "I can't" or, "It's too hard." They use their skills to the limit, and if these aren't enough, they know how to get the extra skills or information they need.

Every summer at the station we had our share of eager students, all determined to be Barbara Walters at the very least. There was an obvious difference between those running on resourcefulness and those just plodding along, coddling their dreams.

Most of our students had some talent, some yearning; but only the blessed few had resourcefulness. The days were full of scenarios like this: "Please go and get me a couple of clips from the film library on the second floor."

Some of the students would bolt out the door like dogs out of a kennel. Others would stand there and shuffle their feet. "Where's the library?" they'd ask. "How do I get the film? Where's the second floor?"

Those you could cross off your list: They were the ones who would come back with one clip and the excuse: "That's all I could find." Their resourceful peers, like Janey, whose T-shirt slogan "Not A Quitter" summed up her whole attitude to life, would return with five clips and ask for another job.

Being resourceful increases your confidence and self-esteem by proving you have ability, courage, and the skills to cope with and master the unexpected.

If resourcefulness has a cousin, it's perseverance, which can command reserves of stamina you don't believe you have. You do.

I've been called an "overnight success," and I am if the night is eighteen years long! It's a long way from being the voice of a shredded wheat to being a TV talk show host. The number of people who have asked me how to get started in show business could supply all the extras for a remake of *Cleopatra* or *Ben Hur*. I always tell them about the slog of making the rounds of directors and casting agents and audition calls. They are all fired up with enthusiasm, but maybe one—and I mean one—has the perseverance to stick it out and make a mark in this business.

People see you only in your present state of success; they don't see or even want to know about the black struggle to get there.

We all envy successful people, but we sure don't envy the constant effort behind their success.

Judith Krantz, author of *Scruples* and *Princess Daisy*, told me she had to persevere like crazy to write *Scru-*

ples, her first book. She locked herself in her bedroom for a year just to get it written, and then she faced countless rejections from publishers who wouldn't consider a first manuscript. But she persevered in the face of ego-crushing turndowns—and, of course, triumphed gloriously when the book finally hit the stands and the best-seller lists.

Fighting obstacles is never easy or something one would choose to do, but it is necessary. Think of it as a test of your staying power and inventiveness.

Perseverance pays off, but you have to want what you're after badly enough to make the struggle worthwhile. You have to be hungry enough and determined enough in pursuit of your dream, so make sure you dream big.

Resourcefulness, perseverance, and determination can be a stalwart wall holding back a sea of troubles that threatens to swamp us. These qualities also bail you out when things turn out tougher than even you expected.

A good friend of mine is taking flying lessons. "Whenever I get really discouraged I reread the life of Amelia Earhart," she says. "If Amelia could stick to it given all the obstacles she had to overcome, so can I." In other words, keep your sights on the light ahead and not on the dark tunnel around you.

Most of us find it difficult if not impossible to cultivate perseverance, and no wonder—we live in a "we want what we want when we want it" world.

Gratification is almost instant for many of our senses. We go to two-hour movies where the conflicts of world wars and stormy relationships spanning four generations are resolved in 120 minutes. We read sagas of entire communities spanning two centuries while on a one-week getaway to Bermuda. We eat instant food, drink instant coffee, and can have instant lovers—few people on earth can't go out the door and find an agreeable male or female to take home for the night if they're not too fussy.

We're all used to things being done quickly, efficiently, instantly, or not at all. To labor at something that's going badly, that is straining and draining us, requiring unexpected effort and patience, tries us in a way it didn't try our grandmothers in their less electric society.

I've heard businessmen around my dinner table complain they can't fill available jobs.

"You must be crazy," I've said. "There are hundreds of people unemployed out there."

"But not the right kind of people, Micki," they tell me. "We need resourceful, ambitious, get-ahead types; we don't believe they exist anymore."

A friend of mine has recently fired her umpteenth personal secretary for that same lack of resourcefulness. If one airline was booked, it never occurred to her to try another and another and another until she got a seat. Oh, she'd do it if asked; my friend just didn't want to be always giving her pages of instructions on how to get through the day! ("Put your hand on the doorknob and turn it slowly to the right; pull the door toward you; walk through.")

Successful people prize those twins—resourcefulness and perseverance—because they are signs of an inner fire they recognize. They should. They have it themselves.

For women who aren't sure what other skills they have or who have yet to acquire skills, these two qualities are an unimaginable boost up the ladder of getting what you want.

Whatever else you learn to do, if you blaze with resourcefulness you will stand out like a neon sign in a field of twenty-five-watt bulbs.

Keeping on with anything—a rocky relationship, a difficult job, a personal problem that's eating at your peace of mind, all those things that demand strength from you—may sometimes make you feel like sinking under the load and quitting. Don't. Call on some good friends or lovers or colleagues to "portage" your load until you're steady on your feet again. It isn't weakness to have a support system. The best athletes in the world have coaches. You don't have to keep doing what you're doing all alone; you just have to keep doing it.

• A Support System

After three auditions and one screen test for a leading role in a major TV series, I got the call telling me I didn't get the part. Did I lock myself in my house and howl and storm for days? Of course not. I locked myself in my girlfriend's house and howled and stormed for days.

What are friends for? They're there to listen to your rage, to mop up tears, to comfort, cajole, and love you— just pour the love into us when some rat or the world in general has drained it all out.

Everybody, but everybody, needs a support system.

It doesn't have to be an elaborate network of fifty people. In fact, it probably shouldn't be: How many people can you realistically be close to?

It can be one or two good friends, a mate, a relative. As long as it's someone who loves you, cares for you uncritically and deeply, it doesn't matter. He/she/they must listen with affection and sympathy and not belittle your problems. They must accept you, flaws, warts, horror stories and all.

That's a lot to ask from one person, which is why I, and a lot of others, spread the support around a little. That way if one of your supporters joins the rat's team, your whole system won't collapse.

There are parts of my life I share only with Leonard, and it's to him I turn for advice and comfort. But time shared with a dear female friend allows me to express different aspects of myself in different ways.

Not everyone is as lucky as I am.

So if you don't have a friend you can tear your heart and hair out in front of, hire one. I mean a therapist.

When my marriage was sinking in a stormy sea, I was

taking a university course in which the professor was also a psychiatrist. I asked him if he could recommend a good marriage counselor. "Ah," he said. "Let me give you the name of the psychiatrist who helped me through my nervous breakdown." Now there was someone who understood!

If you feel this route isn't for you (too much like a plunge into cold water from a fifty-foot diving tower), you still don't have to battle on alone.

Every community has self-help groups for victims of unhappy marriages, widowhood, abuse, rape, or just plain loneliness.

Uh-huh, I hear you say, those people are "weird" or "losers." That's really dead-end thinking. Like you (like all of us), these people have been tossed around by life and are looking for a lifeline. Only a fool would choose to drown rather than reach out for help.

• Self-Discipline

Ugh! That's the only way to describe such a stuffy, un-attractive word as "self-discipline." It dredges up images of eating spinach because it's good for you, muscular gym teachers forcing you over hurdles, and piteous denials from dieters in the face of chocolate mousse.

But this quality is one of the best fortifications a woman can possess. Self-discipline is crucial, whether it's applied to acquiring a skill or losing weight. Not only does it get you through your immediate challenge, it's also a rod of strength to lean on as you go through life.

Margaret Trudeau once told me that Pierre swam fifty-nine laps of the pool every morning—never fifty-eight and never sixty, always fifty-nine. Now that's discipline, and it's run through everything PET has done in his personal and professional career.

It's so much easier to quit anything that's going wrong or getting too tough: a job, a course, a relationship, a new challenge. I've known plenty of people with the philosophy: If it's unpleasant, run. But what they may have saved themselves in pain, they have also lost in satisfaction. Self-discipline is a reserve for tough times, but if you're out of practice, it will be harder to haul it up when it's needed.

It's something I've cultivated, and, like a vitamin pill, I use it every day. When I'm jogging, there are many days I'd like to quit at seven laps. My legs are like lead, my chest is heaving, and I'm panting like a St. Bernard after a trip up the Matterhorn. I could quit at seven laps and no one would know; no one is watching me. But I make myself go eight because I'm disciplined, because it's too easy to quit. Like every other discipline, you have to keep this one in shape through regular use.

Always I tell myself as I pant, jog, pant, jog around that eighth lap that if I don't need self-discipline here on the track this morning, I may need it this afternoon in the studio.

Self-discipline makes me finish the things I don't want to finish. It proves I can do something for myself, not just because someone is judging me. That's important for my self-esteem: to know I can do it for me alone.

My favorite story that illustrates how backbone shoots through an entire life involves young athletic stars. I interviewed these dedicated youngsters as they got up at five a.m. to train for two hours before school and again at the end of the school day. It was a schedule that demanded stamina and discipline from kids under fifteen, one that most adults couldn't match.

I watched them at the track in the chilly morning air, driving themselves, struggling with pain and limitations. What about in the classroom? What did the daily discipline and struggle do for their academic work?

"What are your marks like?" I asked them.

Invariably the reply was the same: Straight A's.

The discipline, concentration, backbone, and commitment permeated their young lives.

After that I did nine laps of the track.

• Get Smart

There are three kinds of smarts, and you'll need all of them.

There are book smarts, which come from books (natch) and courses and magazine articles; there are people smarts, which include networking and role models and friendly contacts; and there are street smarts, which are the kind you get from experience.

Smarts don't come all at once. It's up to you to pursue them and fit the bits and pieces together until you have the ammunition to get out there and start working and fighting for what you want.

Let's look at these in detail:

Books   My library shelves are bursting with books that tell you everything you want to know about cleaning your nasal passages, finding your G spot, stuffing a baked potato, meeting men, and how not to go up the corporate ladder on your back. Just name a subject, and chances are there's a book on it on my shelves.

There is no excuse for not finding out everything about your special interest. Books give you all the background, the history, the case studies, the pros and cons of the subject. And they can be a practical help. My good friend Norah got her first job in television because she could speak the studio lingo—"fade to black," "trucking a camera," "countdown"—when she went for her interview. She picked it up from a book. She'd never set foot in a television studio until the day she applied for the job, but the producers felt comfortable with someone who "spoke their language." Whatever interests you, read, read, and read some more about it.

People   Life's major transactions involve people, so don't think you can be stuffy or shy or ignore them. Treat them right, with a maximum of respect and a minimum of gossip, and (probably) they'll treat you right, too. I've been in my business long enough to know everybody in town. One of the brightest young directors who's now the new darling of the press used to be the coffee gofer at the production company I worked for. When he's looking for a glamorous, fortyish lady for his next picture, won't I be glad I never complained that the coffee was always cold!

Don't think you have to know a thousand people—just one, the right one, will do. Knowing the one (right) person landed me a part in summer stock, and knowing one (right) agent got me in a string of commercials.

Okay, so how do you find these "right" people who can help your career? They don't just happen along. You have to seek them out. People who know people are the kind who are always planning ahead, looking for contacts, laying groundwork, keeping up contacts. You have to do the same. For instance, you meet a woman at a friend's party who works in a field you're interested in. You can chat and drift away quickly to chat with someone else, or you can turn on the charm and dazzle her. Get her phone number. Suggest lunch. Call and make that lunch date. Nothing may come of it for months, but one day she may remember you were interested in fashion or public relations or advertising or whatever it is, and she's shorthanded. Here comes the call: Would you like to give it a try?

Don't try this technique just once and sit around waiting. Do it everywhere you go, with everyone you meet. It's up to you to build a network of contacts. I keep an address book filled with the names and phone numbers of every person I've met in or related to show business over the past twenty years (I'm not kidding, every single one of them), and I use it all the time.

A lot of timid people are afraid they'll be accused of "using" others. That's nonsense. I used to suffer from that fear myself, but I reversed my thinking; now I consider I'm doing them a favor by giving them the opportunity to use wonderful little me.

Making the rounds of agents and casting directors used to make me feel sick, I loathed it so much. I would arrive on their doorstep nervous and fidgety and begging (well, practically begging) for a job.

Then I turned it around. As I trudged up another flight of dingy stairs, I'd keep saying, "I'm giving you the chance to hire fabulous Micki Moore and make your production a success, you lucky thing." When my attitude changed, so did theirs. It was no longer, "Don't call us, we'll call you." It was, "Let's have coffee." If you're dragging yourself along, wishing you weren't there, others start to wish the same thing. You have a right to try for success. You have a right to try every way and every person who can help you, so don't apologize for your ambition. Chin up and get marching!

Actually, powerful people enjoy assertiveness and forwardness in others. They respect it. They recognize hunger, beacuse they were hungry once, too. That's how they got to the top. That's how you'll get to the top, too.

Street Smarts Being bopped around by life is just part of getting street smart. Sure, you might get hurt a little. When you don't get the job because of someone's Machiavellian machinations, when you weren't quick enough to see that the way to the boss's heart was not through hard work but through flattery, when a friend who had promised help on a special project lets you down in a big way—it's a reality that touches everybody's life. Accept it, forget about taking it personally, let it toughen you up, and move on.

I have worked for bosses who have been impossible. In one case the underhandedness and dirty tricks were too much, and I just left. But I tucked away the experience, and one day—maybe when I'm playing Medusa—it will prove invaluable!

In a business like mine, it would have been easy to become a ruthless person. I'm not, although I've been known to give a "soft left hook" when it was deserved.

But I haven't set out to destroy people. Some do. Know it, lament it if you must, but be prepared. You can't always avoid these types. It was difficult to go through school without a confrontation with the playground bully, so you'd better know how to face up to them.

None of these ways of getting wisdom happen magically overnight. They are part of an ongoing process of getting smarter and learning to protect yourself while getting what you want. They are part of the process of self-fulfillment. That process has to start someday, so it might as well be today. Fasten your boxing gloves, ladies and gentlemen, please.

• *Acquire a Skill*

If there's one thing I hear constantly from women (after: "I hate my thighs"), it's: "I'm not good at anything."

If that's you talking—get good!

Nothing is stopping the woman (or the man, for that matter) who feels inadequate or underskilled from returning to university, taking a night course, applying for on-the-job training, or reading her brains out to teach herself.

The only thing holding you back is lack of perseverance and self-discipline.

Oh, it's not that, Micki, you say, it's just that I haven't had a chance yet. I know you're successful, but you've had lots of opportunities.

Well, let me tell you the secret of success: *Opportunity always comes disguised as hard work.*

Hard work means you never stop learning, never stop challenging yourself or acquiring fresh skills and experiences. I have learned things I never dreamed of, because I pushed myself in new directions, often creating my own opportunities.

A few years back a fellow actor and myself were doing a stand-up comedy routine together. We couldn't find any material we really liked, so we wrote our own. I wouldn't have thought of myself as a comedy writer, ever. But know what? We were pretty good, and the material we hadn't used when the act broke up we sold to other comedians.

Skills give you confidence, and developing one very good skill can be your ticket to success. People who rise to the top, though they may be good at several things, are usually thoroughly accomplished in one particular area. The key is to find yours. All skills are important, and it's so much easier to build one skill on top of another until one day you find you are atop a mountain of knowledge and ability.

At CITY-TV one superbright secretary was bored with her job and wanted to try something new. Her reputation as a worker was good, and management let her train as a video tape editor. She was fast and good and dependable and resourceful. Management then promoted her to studio director. She worked her buns off and was excellent. Today she's a producer, and she's good at that, too. (Incidentally, she met her future husband when they edited blue movies together.)

This is a true story. The woman isn't Superwoman, and she could have sat behind her secretary's desk for another decade moaning about her job. Instead she decided to test herself and cemented one skill on top of another until she had a whole repertoire of talent, experience, and confidence to draw from.

What's really important is to remember that this woman never for one moment thought she couldn't do something just because she'd never done it before. Okay, if you can't debone a chicken, maybe you should cross "surgeon" off your list of goals. Likewise, if you can't work a calculator you may have to forget accountancy—but don't say no until you've tried!

We don't know how far our talents will stretch (or what new talents will emerge) until we plunge in and try. So try everything that interests you: Read all about it, study it with passion, feed your interests, update your skills. The only person saying you can't is you.

• Self-Acceptance and Self-Trust

You know the feeling—you walk out of the interview/job/audition/date ready to jump off a building rather than live with the shame of your performance.

Many's the time I've kicked myself all the way home for a lousy effort; I should have done this, said that, stood this way, laughed instead of frowned, been more serious and less giggly. I've taken this tale of woe to friends, family, lovers, kids, the meter reader, the dog, anyone who would listen to how badly I'd done, how stupid I was, how big, big, big my mistake was.

Looking back now, I realize *I did the best I could with the equipment I had*. I see how much time, energy, and emotion I wasted beating and kicking myself over something I couldn't change.

But before I could see that, I had to learn to trust myself and accept myself. It all falls back on that good, solid foundation: self-esteem. I still go to auditions and don't get the job, but it doesn't destroy me anymore. I know it's not a reflection of me or my talent but a combination of things I can't control: Maybe the director once had an unhappy affair with a brunette and he hates them.

In my profession, acceptance is something you learn early. If you can't accept what and who you are, you're headed for the emotional and mental shredder. Everything (in this business, anyway) is against you, so you have to be for you.

Consider the acting profession: It's loaded with rejection, employment is sporadic, there's little control in decision making (you can't force Stephen Spielberg to make a movie that's a perfect vehicle for you), and no matter how good you are, they can always find someone better-looking, with longer legs or the right accent.

There is only one way to do things whatever your business is—the best way you can, every time, with every ounce of talent, trust, confidence, and ability you can muster.

I am a very intense person. I just don't know how to do things in half measures. I do things with everything I've got or not at all, which is why, before I learned to trust myself, my failures were so devastating—every ounce of energy went into failing like a pro! I've been accused of living with too much pressure, but I believe that if you don't test yourself, push yourself, and risk everything from time to time, you'll never learn to trust your abilities, because you'll never know what they are. I also learned to stop wishing for what I don't have and start trusting and concentrating on what I do.

Now that's a major hang-up. Too many people look at the competition and say: If only I had that. I wish, I wish ... I say: Forget what other people have in terms of looks, talent, ability, and personality and work on what you have, what is uniquely yours. Treasure your talents and show them to the world and keep telling yourself that "life consists not of holding good cards but of playing the ones you've got well."

It isn't only professionally that women must learn to trust themselves. How many are confident in love? I know, and I bet you know, women who make the same mistakes with different men over and over again. They follow up these mistakes with claims of never trusting a man again, never falling in love again, never trusting themselves again.

Nothing could be more fatal to romance than a lack of trust. Trust is a half-instinctive, half-learned quality that depends on mutual give-and-take, so the big lesson is: Trust nobody, and nobody will trust you.

My friend Kathryn, so brilliant in business, so blind in personal affairs, is always trapping herself this way.

"I trust the man deeply at first, and he always makes a fool of me and leaves," she complains. "Every time I say the same thing: 'I'll never trust again, it's the only way not to get hurt.'"

It's also the only way not to get loved.

If Kathryn were honest with herself, and God knows a legion of her friends have tried to make her face up, she'd admit she always falls for the same guy—slick, footloose, a good-timer, someone obviously fighting any kind of commitment.

But her trust, Kathryn says, has been shaken so many times, she no longer trusts her own judgment.

Of course, before she can honestly face and defeat the self-fulfilling prophecy of failed relationships, she has to learn self-acceptance. It's the most difficult trust relationship to form. We have armloads of forgiveness and understanding for others, but rarely do we have an ounce for ourselves. We are willing to forgive our best friend's selfishness and carelessness, but we kill ourselves with remorse over a little personal indulgence. You can forgive and forget and even fall in love with a man you know is a liar, but you shrivel up with self-contempt because in a moment of weakness you gossiped about your best friend. You shake your head fondly over your daughter's, or husband's, or lover's laziness on weekends, but you hate yourself for not doing ten more things than are already on your MUST DO list.

Hundreds of women are stewing in this same predicament, and hovering over all of them I see an image of the C.P.—the Critical Parent.

Okay, I'm not going to lay all the blame at our parents' door (don't forget I'm one, too, and I can imagine what my kids have to say about me), but some of it sits on the welcome mat.

When a challenging, difficult, or demanding situation surfaces, out pop these scolding, impossible-to-please Mom and Dad figures who are never satisfied no matter how hard you try.

I was the kind of schoolkid who always got nine A's and one B. The question at report card time was always, "So why the B?"

Self-doubters (and who hasn't been this way) become their own Critical Parent. "That was a stupid thing to do," they say to themselves in C.P. style. They constantly criticize themselves for not being good enough and not measuring up.

I think of the woman who phones her mother every night of her life at 5:30 p.m., and then one day she's held up in traffic. At 6:30 she calls. "Hello stranger," Mom says.

Naturally, self-doubters tell all their dreadful errors to friends, so the friends can join in and echo the litany of failures and faults.

The answer to being followed through life by a Critical Parent is to just STOP and retire the character, as they say on the stage. When you make a mistake, keep it to yourself; the world will not even notice what you've done (or not done).

When your boss makes a blooper at the annual general meeting, do you think he publishes it on the staff bulletin board? When Katherine Hepburn fluffs a line on Broadway, do you think she takes out an ad in *Variety*? When some woman finally says "No" to Warren Beatty, do you think he'll rent a billboard above the Hollywood hills? (He won't, but the woman might.) As someone once said, "Men enjoy confessing their triumphs; women are happier analyzing their failures."

When you mess up, don't send out formal announcements. If it's so big it blots out the sun, the world will find out by itself, without your help. If it's anything smaller, why snitch on yourself?

When high-powered businessmen make huge and costly errors, they don't hold them up for public scrutiny. Either they aren't mentioned, like a burp at a state dinner, or they're transformed into amusing party stories, and the teller of such tales is saluted for his stylish, self-deprecating humor!

Frankly, life asks—demands—that we take big chances at times. And big chances are loaded with the risks of big letdowns. They don't matter. I'll tell you what does: that you never lose your capacity for trying and trusting yourself to try.

People who doubt themselves stop trying and in a sense stop living life to its fullest, richest, demanding best.

• Get Organized

Need a lesson in organization? Borrow mine. A Los Angeles producer was in town auditioning women for a TV series. Everything I needed for the audition I had stashed in my blue tote bag the night before: script, résumé, and glossy pictures, especially printed up at enormous expense for this one job.

In the producer's office, while he and about twelve assistants to the assistants looked on, I unzipped the tote, smiled winningly, and pulled out—a handful of dirty underwear!

My God! This was my husband's laundry that he was going to drop off on his way to work, and this was *his* tote—my script was out getting starched, and, frankly, I wished I was, too.

"That's very good, Miss Moore," the producer said. "But we're not doing magic acts in this show."

Believe me, if they had been, I'd have gone for a disappearing act.

Since that dreadful morning I have got organized. I write myself notes, I write lists, I label everything (laundry and photographs), I plan far ahead, and I leave nothing to chance. And I am not alone.

In six years of interviewing hundreds of successful women on my show, the one thing they shared was organization. They put the army to shame. Shirley Conran, author of *Lace*, and Diane von Furstenberg, fashion and cosmetic entrepreneur, keep running lists and memos. They and many others delegate like mad, assigning staff, secretaries, and family members their duties and responsibilities.

Okay, so few women can do it on so grand a scale, but every woman can do it. How big does the scale have to be not to take dirty laundry to an audition?

Organization is the key to survival for every woman. Working women balancing family and career need it just to get out the door in the morning. I tell you all, get a time management book, keep a desk diary at home as well as at work, hire a cleaning woman, and plan your home life the way you plan at the office. Share the chores and errands and lower your perfectionist standards about domestic chores—but more about that in a later chapter.

Lack of organization can scuttle the best ideas. Take my friend Barbara. To hear her talk, you'd think she has only to snap her fingers to reap the profits of her brilliant inventiveness. Fabulous new ideas for business ventures just roll into her head every day. Last week it was licorice-and-mango-flavored gourmet popcorn; this week it's discount ballgowns. Each new enterprise seems sure to take off, and the profits from mint-and-Amaretto tacos just have to mount up enough to buy one teensy Mercedes.

But Barbara's line is always, "I know it's a great idea, but I don't have time to work on it right now."

In fact, Barbara always has seventeen great ideas on the go, and none of them ever comes to fruition. She's pulled in so many directions at once that her energy gets fragmented and nothing gets done.

Ideas are great, but not if you refuse to take the time to organize and plan enough to get them off the ground. Barbara needs concentration, focus, and organization in spades! The greatest plans in the world are stillborn unless you can organize them into life.

All the best ideas I ever had became real only when I made the effort to clear the decks and organize to put them into action.

Organization time is investment time, and like most investments, it pays off.

• Build Your Own Cocoon

Every place I've ever lived in has been a reflection of

how I felt about myself and the world.

In my crazy and compulsive twenties, the rooms of our house glowed in hot neon pinks and greens and blazing orange. When my marriage fell apart in my thirties, I moved to a tiny (fifteen-feet-wide!) box that convention dictated should be plastered in white, off-white, and white-white. Unconventional me created a bedroom of soft, cloudy blues and pale orange: very dreamy and very seductive! This was my cheap, chic period (no money, lots of imagination). I made all the pillows and cushions out of old dresses and silk scarves; draperies were bedsheets; flowerpots were inverted lampshade frames. The walls were covered with semi-antiques (junk that I had gathered and collected over the years, each thing representing a memory, a fantasy, an exciting moment from my life). Today I live in what I'd call my dream house. Its curved walls are painted in pretty pinks and peaches, and the atmosphere just oozes the calm, stability, and lovingness of my present relationship.

Always a stranger could walk into any place I lived and tell something about the woman who inhabited it.

And that's important. Home should be your refuge, your security base, your cocoon where you can wrap yourself away from the world. I adore that line of Robert Frost's—"Home is the place where, when you have to go there, they have to take you in"—because it's so true. And that's what every woman's home should be. Even though today a woman's life doesn't always revolve around the home, it still has to be the friendly, welcoming heart of her life.

It doesn't have to be a mansion—we're talking here about a home for the heart. Sometimes the things we bring to any four walls and a floor, to any bland hotel room, make it home, because they speak of love and comfort and familiarity. They create the "home" we carry with us.

I remember helping an actress friend pack for a three-month road tour. Like many actresses, her notion of home was a suitcase and a door with a lock on it, yet that day she revealed that there was a special ingredient to every home-away-from-home she'd ever lived in.

Sorting through a mound of clothes, suitbags, and makeup, I found a huge plastic bag with a grubby old quilt sticking out of it.

"Are you dropping this off at a second-hand store?" I inquired, stuffing the disreputable-looking thing farther into the bag.

She was shocked.

"That's my QUILT," she said. "I never go anywhere without it. I've had it since public school. I couldn't sleep in a strange bed without it."

My friend's feelings of security, warmth, and comfort were wrapped up in that faded old thing. Nor is my friend unique. A businessman friend of Leonard's always takes a book of Robbie Burns's poetry to out-of-town conventions—it's not just that he likes the poems, but they remind him of sitting by the fire in his den with his very special lady. That romantic atmosphere "travels" with the book. Actress Pia Zadora turns every luxury hotel room she stays in into a mini-gym with floor-to-ceiling mirrors, weights, and exercise mats; a girlfriend of mine at university always packed her old flannel nightie when she traveled (which she stuffed into a bottom drawer if a man materialized) to snuggle off to sleep in. I know a grande dame of the fashion world who never travels anywhere without her own teapot (brown, patterned china, four-cup) and her own cup and saucer. Such are the personal possessions we carry through life to make the unfamiliar friendly.

Even within their homes women need a special place that is all theirs, and I don't mean the kitchen. I mean the room that's too small for an extra bedroom, the attic, the den, anywhere you can retreat to and lick your wounds or daydream undisturbed.

With so many women today juggling families and careers, they more than ever need to know there's a place indisputably theirs that they can fill with all their favorite things—flowers, magazines, an easel and water-colors—whatever they need to soothe their soul. My retreat is a tiny room with a bay window overlooking the garden, and nobody, not even the cat, disturbs me there. Your place is a private part of you, so make it beautiful. Decorate it in your favorite colors; fill it with fresh flowers or music or whatever gives you quiet pleasure.

In some households the luxury of a private place is just that—an unattainable luxury. Don't let that stop you from having a dreaming time to yourself. Create it for yourself with time instead of space. Tell your mate that every Thursday and Saturday from seven until nine in the evening (or whatever times suit your lifestyle) are for you and that the running of the household, the children, the chores and grinds of daily living will have to fall on other shoulders.

Another thing: I've always had a lock on the door of my special room. It sounds harsh, but you'll be shocked at how many people assume that when you say: "Keep out," it doesn't mean them. Show them you mean it and end the argument forever. You're not being a hermit or ignoring your loved ones; you're just investing in a little personal time to recharge and get "centered" again.

Before you can go out and face the world you have to face yourself. These quiet, private moments of peace, reflection, and well-earned indulgence make the facing up easier.

• Getting Together Your Survival Kit

So there you have it: a complete survival kit for the mind and body. Shall we go over it one more time?

Build yourself a cocoon to relax and escape from the world, but when you go out don't forget to take a *sense of humor* with you so you won't be soured and defeated by life's downs. (The ups you can handle.) Build *self-acceptance and self-trust* so you can depend on yourself and not on the approval of others.

Cultivate *intuition* so you'll really know yourself and believe in your own decisions.

Nurture *resourcefulness* to pull yourself out of the stickiest situations and *perseverance* to keep you at it when the going gets tough (and it will).

Build skills to light the path for you and open doors to success and *smarts* to protect you and help you achieve new conquests.

Work at *self-discipline* to build your character and make you see everything, not just the nice, easy things, through to the end.

Get organized so you have the time to enjoy your accomplishments and develop *a support system* to pick you up and love you when a crisis hits.

With all this going for you, can success be far behind?

III

Outwitting Your Female
Conditioning

There are times when I want to go out with a bag over my head. No, my daughter Lisa is not at it again! No, it's not time to retouch the roots. It's my face: People recognize it. Because I've appeared in their living rooms daily, they feel they know me.

A perfect stranger stopped me on a busy downtown street and asked, "Do you know who you are?"

I did when I woke up this morning, I thought, but before I could answer, the man continued: "I watch your show every day. I've got to talk to you. You won't believe what's happening in my life. I'm having an affair with my mother-in-law."

A fan is a fan; I always try to listen and help, but a looney tune is also a looney tune. "Sorry, gotta dash," I shouted over my shoulder as I leaped onto a passing streetcar and got off a block later.

Under the dryer at the hairdresser, there is no escape. But then, I wouldn't really want one. I have some of my best conversations with other women there. One day when I emerged from a roaring dryer, a determined-looking matron sat herself down beside me.

"Micki," she said, "you've got to help me. I have two daughters—one has just become a lawyer, and the other has just got married. And I'm so worried."

"About which one?" I asked, since they both seemed to be doing all right.

The woman looked surprised. "About the lawyer, of course," she said. "The other will be fine: she's got a husband."

I checked the calendar. Yes, we were definitely in the 1980s, but some of us still have a lot of catching up to do.

This woman, caring, concerned parent though she may be, has bought every message our society is selling about what it means to be female. These are the influences that, consciously and unconsciously, help make you female—or someone's version of it.

Little girls are sugar and spice. (In that case when, and how, can I get angry?)

Someday my Prince will come. (Mine did; he left after a few years, too.)

A woman's place is in the home. (Who decided that I was born with an innate knowledge of bathroom cleansers?)

If you're too smart you'll never get a man, and if you don't have a man you're not a real woman. (But what kind of man would I get?)

If you're too successful you'll end up alone. (Do I always have to be less so he can be more?)

You will never be thin enough, smell good enough, be beautiful enough. (Will I ever measure up?)

These messages are subtly veiled threats to you and your self-esteem. They whittle away at your confidence, causing doubts and fears; they are designed to keep you in your place and stop you from moving ahead. Sadly, they often work.

• *You Don't Have to Buy What They're Selling*

As a teenager I used to hunt through the women's magazines for stories about successful career women. Although I had dreams and aspirations, I always checked the end of the article first to see if they were also married and had children. This was the only kind of happily-ever-after I could possibly imagine.

The woman at the hairdresser's had swallowed all the messages, although at least one of her daughters hadn't.

Ignoring the messages or creating new ones isn't easy when much of our society reinforces them so strongly. There is not yet a place in women's mythology for the powerful, assertive, tough, independent woman who is also unquestionably desirable. And it is our desire to be desired that usually holds us back. If you want a man, young woman, you have to be submissive, dependent, and unable to face life alone. Otherwise, what is there for a man to do? (Smart ones have discovered a few other things.)

If men are hard to get, the thing that ropes them in—youth—is hard to keep. Hollywood keeps this eternal threat hanging over our heads. Fred Astaire or Cary Grant may be able to age gracefully and sexily, but their leading ladies had to pack up their wrinkle cream and switch to character roles. Grant went through four decades of leading ladies—Katherine Hepburn in the 1930s, Ingrid Bergman in the 1940s, Grace Kelly in the 1950s, and Sophia Loren in the 1960s—and no one questioned his right to always be the suave romancer.

When I was in my teens, it was an accepted "fact" that women peaked at thirty, were over the hill at forty, and were finished by fifty. Men, of course, just matured nicely.

The second part of the age threat, of course, was: "You older women had better behave, or he'll trade you in for a younger model."

One of the many reasons that Jane Fonda has become a role model is that, being such a crusader for fitness, she redefines our image of an "older woman." Said Jane in a recent interview, "I don't have any desire to lie about my age. If you're healthy, no matter what age you are, you have sexual stamina, desire, flexibility, and all the things that go into an active sex life. Not only do middle-aged women have to be present on the screen and on television, they have to be there as sensual people."

But we don't give up our myths in one generation.

My own children have rushed to the defense of my "old age." Daughter Lisa arrived home from school one day and confided in hushed tones that all the kids wanted to know how old I was. "But don't worry, Mom," she said with true daughterly love. "I didn't tell them!"

Another time my son, Lance, brought his friends home while I was sitting at the kitchen table sipping coffee and reading over a script. The boys stared at me for some time in respectful silence. Finally Lance said, grabbing my arm, "Tell them, Mom—tell them you didn't have a face transplant!"

After I'd stopped laughing—and assuring the young message-makers that a woman in her thirties could look okay without trickery—I couldn't help wondering if these boys would remember as they got older that they had found an assured, confident, older face attractive and pleasing. Would they pass that message on to the women in their lives, and would the women be confident enough to receive and believe it?

For most women, their most influential role model is Mother. Some mothers have passed on the old messages in heaps and bundles because of their own fears. They have been trapped themselves by the mythology and by economic restraints, and they have had few choices in their lives. New paths being forged by their daughters look a lot like treason.

I overheard a mother talking to her grown daughter, who was struggling with unwanted independence (a divorce). "Maybe things will get better if I go out and get a job," the woman was saying. "Maybe someday I'll meet another man, a nice one, who'll treat me better."

"Come off it," her mother snapped. "You're thirty-five, with two kids. Who'd want you?"

Dependence, the need for approval, enforced docility—these all fill a prescription for failure.

And don't count on those closest to you to help you become self-reliant.

When my husband and I separated, he kept saying he was looking for that sweet, shy little girl he married. Whatever happened to her? he mourned. I told him: She grew up. I was glad to get rid of her; she was vapid, insecure, and inexperienced. Why would I want to hang onto her?

What had grown in her place was a woman who had substance and character and independence, who could meet a man on equal terms. My husband found that uncomfortable. Sometimes men have to grow up and outwit their conditioning, too. (It isn't easy for anybody out there in the big, bad world.)

Just recently I found myself in the position of being a referee between two very good friends. The younger of the two, a pale blonde in her mid-forties, was feeling the first stirrings of independence now that her children were grown.

"I haven't worked since I was first married," she confessed. "But I'd like to do something now. I have so much time."

"Come off it, Judy," her "friend" piped up. "You can't compete in the business world. You're too old."

I tried to smooth things over. "It takes a lot of organizational skill to run a household, and I know you've done committee work with volunteer groups," I said. "Could you use any of that experience to get you started?"

"Probably, if I took some kind of upgrading course," Judy said, her face lighting up with the possibility.

"Oh, really," came her friend's parting shot before she left to join a more "sensible" group of gossipers. "Pamela went back to school, remember, and three months later her husband moved out."

Judy looked upset; this wasn't the place for a lecture on assertiveness, but I thought one little story might inspire her.

"I know a woman who was in your position a year ago," I told her. "Her best skill was a traditional one—baking. But she turned it into a business, and now she supplies restaurants with the best mocha torte and chocolate mousse cake."

"And her husband?" Judy asked. "How did he take it?"

"He took it!" I said. "Literally! He delivers the cakes!"

She burst out laughing, and I knew she was on her way.

It's too late only if you believe it's too late. Moreover, discovering your skills will give you new faith in yourself. It's time for each of us to stop thinking like a woman and start thinking like a person.

My friend Diana brought along a colleague to one of our monthly let-it-all-hang-out lunches. Over the wine and daily special at our neighborhood restaurant we confess our transgressions, laugh at our mistakes, cry over our latest goofs, and generally do more for our psyches than a dozen visits to a psychiatrist.

Her workmate, Diana said, could use some cheering up. "She's just found out that her husband's having an affair."

I kept stealing glances at Diana's friend throughout the lunch as we chatted about the polite and pleasant things that strangers are allowed to. This woman was nice if unexceptional-looking. She looked a little tired, a little resigned, but she didn't look destroyed by the news of her husband's infidelity.

Eventually the subject came up, and I wasn't prepared for her response.

"I'm sure it's a very painful discovery," I ventured, not wanting to intrude on her feelings, yet not wanting her to think she had to keep silent if she needed to talk.

"It is, but I have no one to blame but myself," she said, her eyes filling with tears. Oh-oh, I thought, here comes the real story: She was unfaithful first, or she told her husband she didn't love him anymore, or she ordered twin beds without telling him.

It was none of those things.

"I'm too old," she said, although she was barely into her forties. "Terrance is a very handsome, young-looking man. He can't help being attracted to younger women and they to him. And I'm overweight and not as pretty as I used to be."

Nothing, I thought, that a weekly exercise class and a visit to a good salon couldn't cure. But curing her self-image would be a more difficult process.

"I gave him everything, and it was never enough," she said with a spark of anger that quickly faded. "Maybe I didn't have enough to give."

This last reflection revealed the source of her trouble.

Like too many other women, she had based her every move and decision on the one question: What will *he* think? She had convinced herself that if she did everything his way, did it all for him, he couldn't help loving her forever.

The more she gave, the more he took. The less she received, the more unhappy she became.

She'd received the message of submission loud and clear from girlhood and knew no other way.

There *is* another way, a way based on *your* needs, not on anyone else's. You don't have to keep buying what they're selling.

When I reentered the singles scene after my marriage folded, I met many men who told me I was fascinating—but they wouldn't want to be married to me. Why, I asked myself (and a hundred girlfriends), was it such a burden for a man to be married to a woman who was intelligent, articulate, and independent? These men said to me, "I love your strength, but I wouldn't want to live with it." They felt it somehow diminished their strength. Of course, I eventually met a man who was smart enough and secure enough to see that it didn't, but I had practically given up by that time. Combined strengths and talents and independent interests make for a relationship layered with richness.

So before taking any action ask yourself: How do I really feel about this? Do I want to do it, does it make me happy? Will I benefit?

This isn't selfishness. It doesn't mean that in loving yourself, you love him less. But you must love yourself enough to look out for yourself in this wicked world. If you don't, why should anyone else? If you put so little value on yourself, how precious can you be to another?

We all care for, protect, and treasure the things we value most—make sure you're one of them.

• Comfortable Traps

Usually we think of traps as painful things that pinch and hurt us. But some of the most dangerous traps are the ones that feel so good we want to stay in them forever. They're cosy and protective, and they keep challenges at bay. Let's look at some of the more familiar ones.

His Success Is My Success For years Joanie used to have hot chocolate and warm socks ready for her family of skiers when they trudged into the cottage after an exhilarating race. Since she took up skiing herself five years ago, her sons have learned to make the cocoa—with a dash of Grand Marnier—for Mom.

There's no doubt about it. Running a race is very different from watching it, however pleasurable the viewing might be. And earning a paycheck is very different from having a portion of it turned over to you. His success it not your success. He is out there living his life, and if you are living as his shadow, you are not living yours.

From the day I was married I worked, but somewhere at the back of my mind (all that conditioning!) I felt that his job was more important than mine. My problems weren't as important as his, his salary meant more (it was certainly bigger), and even when I got really good jobs, people treated my work as a "little hobby." He worked; I dabbled.

And when we split up, all the sense of accomplishment went out the door with him. The "success" of our lives was his, and he took it with him. I felt a big chunk of my life and identity went, too.

Women need work that is theirs. It doesn't have to be an outside job, but it should be something that is demanding, challenging, satisfying, and fulfilling. A good friend of mine paints beautiful, enchanting canvasses, some of which hang in my home, and that is her work.

Having your own money is important, too. Money puts you in a better negotiating position and gives you more control. According to Drs. Pepper Schwartz and Philip Blumstein in their book, *American Couples: Money, Work, Sex*, the money that a working woman brings home earns her power in the household and respect from her partner. Money still determines the balance of power in most relationships.

If you're earning it outside your warm, nesty home, you're learning, too. The experiences and difficulties and rewards of the outside world keep you from becoming stale and dull. Women, as much as men, need challenges, stimulation, and a chance to grow. Unearth your talents and put them to work. Unused things tarnish—and you want to shine, shine, shine!

I Have Everything I Want Here   After I had given a speech on being everything you're capable of being, a nervous young woman approached me. She enjoyed the talk, she said, but she could never do what I do. I don't need to, she said. I'm a wife and mother, and I have everything I need.

Well, I was a wife and mother, too! I needed those things, but I also needed something else, something just for me. Okay, this woman feels she has everything she needs today at twenty-three. But what about at thirty-three and forty-three? (She probably doesn't think she'll ever live to such an old age, but believe me, it happens.) The key word is *now*. Just because you are, for now, out of the hurly-burly business world and concentrating on raising a family (or African violets or angel food cakes), don't assume this will be the only interest in your life forever.

What I'm saying is: Don't put your brain on the shelf.

Don't let your potential lie dormant, because when you do need it—in one, five, or ten years from now—you won't be able to wake it up!

Success is getting what you want. Happiness is wanting what you get. Don't assume the wants and needs and desires won't change.

In her wonderful book *Pathfinders*, which I have pored over during the crises of my life, Gail Sheehy lists the things that give people the greatest sense of well-being in their lives. Making one or two major transitions and meeting those challenges in a positive way are high on the list.

Make sure you always keep your challenge-meeting equipment and talents in top working order, no matter what else is happening in your life.

I Hate Anxiety If you put yourself on the firing line, you get fired at.

In one of the first auditions I went to in New York I was determined to take a big bite out of the Big Apple. A little lick was more like it. I had prepared speeches, a monologue, and a song-and-dance routine. I was willing to stand on my head and sing "The Star-Spangled Banner" if it would get me the job.

Backstage with me and filled with the same hot ambition were about two hundred other young brunettes. By the time my number was called (No. 146), I was revving on adrenalin and chattering with nerves.

The director, seated somewhere in the darkened theater, called out: "Say 'Hello, I'm new in town.'"

I gave it all I had. (It wasn't much.) There was a pause, and then the director's voice floated over the footlights: "Hate her. Next."

Hate me? Next? How could he hate me when he didn't even know me?

I wasn't just fired at. I was shot down in flames before I'd even dusted off my ammunition. Facing the possibility of that kind of rejection causes a wave of anxiety, for sure. But, I told myself as I slouched off sobbing, if I never take a risk, never step out, what am I doing with my life?

I tell women that only three things can happen when they take a risk: One, they'll succeed. Two, they'll fail but survive to try again. Three, they'll have a great story for a book someday.

I'd make a fool of myself, women have told me. I'd just die. So die—and be resurrected! Women who stay in their anxiety-free zones, never testing themselves, never risking anything, will never know their talents and never leave their mark on the world. And one day when they're little old ladies rocking on the front porch and a young woman asks them to talk about their life, they'll honestly be able to answer: What life?

Don't let this be you!

Return to Traditional Values   Just let someone, anyone, trot out this old line and run it up the flagpole, and women everywhere start clicking their heels and saluting like mad as they leap to attention. It calls to them in tunes of glory (someone else's glory, to be sure) that have been pummeled and programmed into them since childhood: A woman is a wife and mother, the nurturer of the family; the reason the world is plagued with famine, pollution, delinquent kids, unemployment, street riots, prostitution, and tooth decay is because women have forsaken traditional values.

Bunk.

What people mean when they call for the "return to traditional values" is that they want to go back to a time when women were powerless.

Yes, women were and still are, I hope, nurturers of their families, but there is more. Personally, I'd work toward a return to strong values. Moral codes are important, especially when you're raising kids, and these codes of behavior and high standards will stay with them through life. But having a mother with interests and pleasures outside her family won't undermine these standards.

I certainly don't regret the way I brought my kids up, and they had a working mom all their lives. Yes, I spent time away from them, but when they needed me I was there. And I didn't do everything I wanted to. There were plays and road shows that I turned down because they would have taken me away from Lisa and Lance for too long.

Today when I look at them I know I did the right thing. I see two mature, well-adjusted, independent young adults who are discovering and enjoying life. And we're friends. Your children are with you always, and you have to be able to face them as adults—I'm happy to face mine.

My son is the kind of young man who lets his mother think he's forgotten her birthday (not even a phone call all day) and then, when she goes out to drown her sorrows at a neighborhood restaurant, sneaks in the house and covers her bed with fresh flowers and a bag of chocolate chip cookies. Now that is a son who really understands and loves his mother!

Do everything you can to provide your family with the best, most positive and nourishing environment, but never forget they are *part* of your life, not all of it.

Letting Others Make Your Decisions   I saw a fascinating interview the other day with three gutsy entertainers: Farrah Fawcett, Cheryl Ladd, and Bette Midler. All three women had just fired their managers and had hired new ones they had personally chosen. All three were taking charge of their lives and careers and pushing in the direction they wanted to go.

A generation ago these women would have been turned out of Hollywood with the golden gates slammed in their faces. Once the studios ran the stars' lives. They invented biographies for them, birthplaces, families, hobbies, and romances. Managers and agents ran them.

But no more. Men got tough first. Women haven't been far behind, as Farrah, Cheryl, and Bette proved. These three learned the hard way that allowing others to make decisions about your life keeps you trapped in dependency.

Of course, it's very comfortable there. If someone else makes the decisions you never have to take the blame when things go wrong, although you're the one who ends up with egg on your face. But the conclusion that Farrah, Cheryl, Bette, and I, and thousands of other self-reliant women, have come to is that the only person who knows what's best for me is me.

The person who is organizing your life for you starts to feel they own it. Why not? They're doing all the work and worrying.

It isn't easy or comfortable to have to wrest control away from someone or fight to keep someone who thinks they should be running your life out of it. I have struggled against parents, a husband, and subsequently several men friends (and some women) who were convinced they knew who Micki Moore was, how she should live, and what she should be.

I am the person I have to live with for the rest of my life, no matter who else is with me. Let me tell you some wonderful news—I own my own soul. And it feels really good.

Emotional Dependency Maybe I still have to reach the outer limits of liberation, but I still have days when I wish I were Cinderella. The pressures, the assignments, the responsibilities pile up on top of me, and I long for a Prince Charming to ride into my life and sweep my problems away (while sweeping me off my tired feet). However, the last White Knight rode off with the unicorn and neither has been seen since, so I pull myself together and cope as best I can.

The plain truth is that there is no one person on

whom we can unload all our worries and responsibilities, although women try. Women long for their princely rescuer to take over their lives, long to surrender their independence, freedom, and power.

This is not only foolish but unhealthy. The only person in the world you can depend on forever is—surprise!—you. There is a nourishing kind of interdependence that springs up in adult relationships that we should cherish; it leads to healthy, rewarding partnerships—more about this later.

The wrong (unhealthy) kind of emotional dependence colors the lives of women like Ava. Whatever her husband asks, she does. Their lives are structured around his demands. What he wants for dinner, they eat; where he wants to vacation, they go; when he wants to party, they show up. He has filled her, like water into an empty pitcher, with his feelings, his opinions, his thoughts. He feeds her dependency (it makes him feel so manly), and she clings to him. Choice is a non-word in their household.

Ava's relationship isn't satisfying, but she describes it as "secure." Nobody could call it "happy."

Economic Dependency   There's another kind of cling-like-plastic-wrap dependency: the kind that involves money.

Alison, an investment counselor I know, gives money management talks to women's groups. During a recent lecture she asked how many of the assembled women knew how much money they and their husbands had in various bank accounts.

Only one woman raised her hand.

How many knew what stocks, bonds, and other investment papers there were?

Again only one woman raised her hand—the same woman.

How many knew what insurance coverage their husbands had, what other financial cushions were tucked away, and how big the household debt was?

Again the same woman raised her hand.

Overcome with curiosity, Alison asked her point-blank why she was the only woman in the room who knew her husband's financial status so intimately.

Because, the woman replied, he died three months ago.

Until then she, like all the other women around her, had had no idea how much money there was and how much was hers.

Many women don't know because they don't want to know. He'll take care of me, he'll provide, they tell themselves, ignoring a fifty per cent divorce rate, accidents, and sudden death. I remember when I went to get "forever and always" engraved on my husband's wedding ring. I ran into a girlfriend who said she'd had the same thing engraved on her husband's band, and now they were divorcing. "That will never happen to me," I thought. Yet a few years later, I was separated, too. Believe me, not one of us marries planning or anticipating divorce.

Some women can't find out about their financial situation because they're married to a Neanderthal who believes women have no right to know. These women have a whole set of other problems besides economic dependency.

But some just refuse to know, because they don't want the responsibility of looking after the finances and because it makes them feel more womanly to be "taken care of."

Feminist Gloria Steinem puts it in chilling terms: "Most women are only one man away from welfare." Could that be you?

• Stop Tap Dancing: Stop Saying, "I'm Sorry"

THWACK! went the tennis ball over the net—a lousy shot.

"I'm sorry," I called to my partner.

THWACK! again, a great shot!

"I'm sorry," I said again.

I'm sorry? Yes, I'm sorry—for bad shots, for good shots, for winning (in case my partner feels bad), for losing (in case I'm not a good enough partner).

Those words—"I'm sorry"—seem to reverberate through my life and the lives of countless other women.

I'm sorry for being late, for not looking so good, for not bringing up the children perfectly, for not being a gourmet cook. I'm sorry for being overweight, for dyeing my hair, for spending so much of your money on this dress, for not spending enough on the car. I'm sorry I've taken time away from you to go to night school; I'm sorry I never finished university so you have to talk down to me. I'm sorry for not being good enough in bed so naturally you turn to somebody else; I'm sorry for being too good in bed so you feel inadequate.

And I'm truly sorry, because "I'm sorry" is ruining my life.

Well, not anymore.

It's taken years, but I have finally learned to stop shuffling my feet in apology, to stop taking on everyone else's mistakes and slipups as well as my own.

Something about women's conditioning makes us all eager to rush forward and take the blame for everything. We're schooled in the female virtues: "good" women are tactful, understanding, and demure. They endure.

Good women love their parents, their spouses, their kids, and they take care of all of them. Their job is to keep everyone happy, and they murmur "I'm sorry" when someone, incredibly, becomes unhappy. Whatever is making that man, that teenager, that parent miserable, it must be their fault. I'm sorry.

You have to toughen up to kick the sorry habit.

Not long after I reentered singledom, vulnerable and innocent like you wouldn't believe, I met a fabulous man. I threw a dinner party to introduce him to my friends. It seemed such a good idea two weeks before, but on the actual day I was a basket case.

What if they hate him? What if he thinks they're stupid or boring? What if the food flops? What if everyone cancels?

I mean, this man wasn't easy to please: He was a very attractive, intelligent stockbroker who worked hard and played hard and whose standards were just slightly below God's.

I spent the day running around buying fresh flowers and slaving over the soufflé dish. I changed the tablecloth and napkins twice. But the real agony was what to wear. Nothing was right, but I picked an old favorite that felt slightly "less wrong."

He arrived ahead of the other guests so we could have a relaxing drink together.

"Micki, I haven't seen that dress before," he said, mixing himself a scotch and soda.

What's wrong with it, I instantly thought. But I said, "Do you like it?"

"It's bright," he said after a pause. Of course it was bright. Everything in my wardrobe from track suits to cocktail dresses is bright—I love vivid colors.

My stomach was slowly rolling over. Did "bright" mean it was too bright? Did it mean he didn't like it? Was he a pastels man? Did I look old in it? Too fat? Too tall?

He said nothing, just sat and frowned slightly into his drink.

So I did what any sensible woman would do—I changed it. My second choice was hardly less bright, but it was a different color. He said nothing, and I was brimming with apologies and misery.

My dinner party was a huge success for everyone but me, who sat under a cloud all night. Something was going on in my heart and head that I didn't like.

At the door he said good night.

I said good-bye.

And I've never said "I'm sorry" again—unless I've committed an appalling crime.

Women throw themselves on the opinions of their men. His glancing look of disapproval, a slight frown creasing his marble brow, is worse than outright criticism. We suffer in silence, eaten up with anxiety. What have I done wrong? What has displeased him? Why isn't he happy? Whatever it is women are eager to assume it's their fault.

In my head I see all these women in a chorus line, tap dancing and shuffling their feet as the men call the tune, shuffling faster and faster as they try harder to please.

When Leonard and I were in the throes of decorating our house, I spent hours searching out fabrics and paint samples and lugging them home for his approval. Between taping ten shows a week, I was in and out of every designer fabric shop in town and looking at stripes, dots, peacocks, and flowers until I was cross-eyed.

Swatches of fabric littered the house.

Our nightly conversations went like this:

"Do you like this one with that one and this one?" I'd ask, running back and forth holding two, three, four samples together for his scrutiny.

"Just so-so," Leonard would say.

"Well, how about this one? It could go in the den if we put this one, that one, and that one in the hall."

"Maybe."

Every response was the same and carried a tone of disapproval. Soon the only thing I wanted to see hanging over the fireplace was Leonard's head!

Finally I took a deep breath and took off my tap shoes.

"Look," I told him. "Here are the fabrics and colors I like. I hope you like them, too. But if you don't, you can either go out and find some you like better or hire an interior decorator. I've done the best I can and won't do anymore."

Leonard said he loved the colors.

How can you tell if you're tapping and shuffling too

fast or if you're just trying to smooth the troubled waters of a relationship? The women who dance the fastest are the ones who are most unsure of themselves. Not hearing their own music, they'll dance to anybody's tune. The shakier a woman's self-concept, the more willing she is to accept an outside judge.

Listen, lady, just throw out those tap shoes once and for all. Throw them at your critics if you want to.

• Parameters—Setting Your Limits

A stranger approaches you at a party, kisses your bare shoulder, and says, "Hi ya, baby." You cringe.

Your best friend tells a very personal story about you, one you shared only with her. You question the friendship.

The new man in your life fails to show up yet again at the restaurant he's picked for dinner. He becomes the ex-man in your life.

You and your man are having a big fight. You each dig deeper into the insult bag, slinging whatever comes up first. The whole nasty scene is upsetting, but it's happened before, and you're covering familiar ground. Suddenly, out of nowhere, your man hits you with a real zinger—an absolutely off limits, deeply wounding accusation or reference to that ex-lover, your extra twenty pounds, or your bad skin. Pow! You are so shocked and stunned you can't respond. You could almost double over with the pain.

What has happened? He has crossed your parameters, the unspoken but powerfully real boundaries you draw around yourself. These are the standards you set to let other people know how you expect to be treated.

He, the stranger at the party, your questionable best friend, and your ex-man have all broken your parameters of self-protection, thereby failing to respect who you are. It happens to everybody. It's certainly happened to me.

So what can you do about it? Some gentle souls say

forgive and forget, some logical types want to reset the barrier and try again, some hurt and hurt until the relationship crumbles.

A lot depends on who said what when and how determined you are to hang onto the relationship. Divorces have resulted from barrier crashing; estrangements in family and among friends have lasted for years, sometimes to the grave!

Then why set limits at all? you ask. Why not have no-holds-barred relationships? After all, we're talking about people you love and trust. We are, indeed, and that's why more than ever we need self-protecting parameters. For me, a primary condition of any relationship has to be mutual respect at all times for each other's limits and boundaries.

It can be very straightforward. When I was dating the campus hero at Ohio State University, I felt I'd really hit the top. He was one of those good-looking, good-at-everything charmers. Shy as I was, I couldn't believe he'd picked me over the other women.

So what was our relationship like? Awful! I was embarrassed when he flirted with other women when I was around; I was mortified when he never introduced me to his men friends; he made dates that were "for sure" unless there was a football practice; and I did things—things he wanted to do—at the last minute with no warning. But I was too scared of losing him to complain about being treated like a little dog.

Of course, I lost him anyway to another starry-eyed woman. If my parameters had been more clearly defined and my courage more in place, I could have told this young Adonis that I resented being treated like a throwaway date and the treatment wasn't good enough for me.

The point of all this ancient history is that if you don't let people know what the limits are and make it clear what transgressions are unforgivable, be prepared to take whatever treatment they're dishing out.

If you don't speak up, the message you are sending

is: "It's okay to treat me any way you want; you can be cruel, selfish, disrespectful. I don't care about my rights as a woman, a person, a lover in this relationship..."

Quite simply, setting parameters is telling people what's right for you. If they love and care for you they'll respect your standards just as you try to respect theirs.

• Why Can't a Woman Be More like a Woman?

What is it about some women that as soon as they get a taste of success or a foot up the ladder, they also get a suit of armor—hard, flinty stuff that makes them hard inside, too. Tough, cold, heartless. I know what they're doing, and so do you if you've worked with one of these gorgons—they're trying to "be like a man."

Men are tough, men are ruthless, men are successful. Women imitate them to get their share of success. But nobody's said that being tough (in that "male" way) is a good thing. Freeing yourself from female conditioning doesn't mean embracing male conditioning instead!

I once worked with a woman whose co-workers labeled her "the woman with the iron fist." She prided herself on operating "tough, just like a man." All her budgets and people were in line; her employees arrived at nine and left at five on the dot. They followed the rules she set, and she stood over them to make sure the job was done her way. There was no room for emotions or sensitivity; she wasn't going to be called a "soft touch." But little did that woman with the iron fist realize that what gains she made in control and efficiency she lost in productivity, morale, and creativity. Yet she almost prided herself on the turnover of staff: they weren't tough enough to meet her standards.

One day it was brought to her attention that the people who weren't tough enough transferred to other departments in the company, where they were soon rising stars. When this was researched, their answers were similar: Even though they hadn't liked all the rules, they could have handled them. But what hadn't been available to them from their iron-fisted manager was empathy when they were handling difficult problems, space to express their own creativity, and some understanding when the rules had to bend.

It's not that she didn't have those qualities—compassion, sensitivity, or understanding—she was just afraid to use them in business for fear of being trapped by her femininity; she was petrified of doing anything soft. She traded stereotypical feminine behavior for stereotypical male behavior in case she might be perceived as weak. Neither type of behavior is totally productive.

Powerful women embrace the concept of androgyny (male-femaleness). They freely express all sides of themselves without regard to whether their behavior is masculine or feminine. They can be tough, analytical, and forceful, and nurturing, sympathetic, and understanding when necessary.

This is what this woman learned. They don't call her the iron-fisted woman anymore. She got in touch with all parts of herself, and now they call her vice-president.

I love that story, because it's true of so many striving women. They have to learn, as I learned, that you must combine the best of both sexes. For years I wasn't getting ahead professionally because I was too emotional, too sensitive, too passive. The men who were getting far ahead of me were harder, more ruthless, more aggressive. They were never modest. They never apologized for their mistakes.

So I drew up my own list to spur me on. I listed all my female qualities and all the male ones, too—I found I had quite a few of those buried under layers of conditioning.

I sum up my androgyny this way:

- I am both active and passive.
- I am both competitive and cooperative.
- I am both a giver and a taker.
- I am both assertive and docile.

• I can stand on my own two feet, but I need to stand next to someone I care about.
• And by becoming independent, I can establish a healthy interdependency.

For too long I drew on all the feminine characteristics while the masculine ones lay dormant. I was over-developed in one area and underdeveloped, almost atrophied, in another. Now I think I've balanced the books pretty well. This balance has given me new confidence and assurance, because now I've twice as much to draw on.

Nor has it hardened or coarsened me. I feel more feminine than I ever have before.

• Don't Put Up with Put-Downs

"Oooh, that's not another spoonful of ice cream going into that cute, fat little face of yours, is it, darling?"

I actually heard some beast of a husband say this to his wife (who did have a fat little face but probably didn't want to be reminded of it) in front of fourteen people at a barbeque.

"I think that's a fabulous dress, even if it is last year's style."

Was my friend trying to be kind and share her fashion savvy when she laid this on me?

Then there was the total stranger who walked up to me on the street one day and said, "Gee, Micki, you're not as fat as you look on TV."

Thanks, buddy.

Put-downs are those little zingers that are short, sweet, effective ways to attack us.

Why do we put up with them? They attack our sensibility, they wound us, they hurt even though they are often delivered under the guise of flattery or amusement. They belittle, they patronize, and sometimes they presume.

I've noticed that the most effective ones are whipped

off by people who are nearest and dearest. Do you really need a loved one to needle you about your thunder thighs or about your new haircut that makes you look like a fourteenth-century serf?

Jules Feiffer called these one-shot put-downs "little murders" because of what they do to your self-esteem, and I've never heard a better description.

It's awkward. On one level those insults and affronts seem too petty to mention. Getting upset over them seems more childish than delivering them in the first place, and yet . . .

"Honey, it's just a joke," is the time-honored excuse usually trotted out after you explain how much these barbs pierce you. How can you say without sounding like such a baby that coming from someone you love and trust, they're just killing?

I used to keep my mouth shut. "Cool down, Micki. Don't make a big deal out of it, don't be a bad sport. He doesn't mean it."

Then why does he say it?

A male tennis partner used to "compliment" me after getting an impossible shot by saying, "Not bad for an old broad."

When I was at the point of bursting a blood vessel, I asked him straight out what he meant.

He stumbled around, shrugged, and finally admitted he meant I was in great physical condition, better than many other women my age.

"Thanks," I said. "Great. So why didn't you say so?" (Now he does or just finds another partner.)

Having endured these little put-downs, I've now re-classified them. They are not harmless little digs: They are often the first step to intimate warfare, and if you don't want a full-scale battle escalating, you'd better act now.

The only reason we put up with them is that our self-esteem is too weak to stand up to them. Gather your courage; speak up and talk back.

You can do it gently. If you don't put the lid on

put-downs, nobody else will. But what about the person who persists in putting you down?

Years back I worked for an employer who started every encounter with an intimidating tactic. "I see you have more lines in your face today," he would say, and that was one of the milder ones. (My *Women and Management* books never prepared me for this one!)

After a few of these I realized the power game he was playing. At the next meeting, staring at my chest, his opening line was, "I see you are perspiring all over your silk blouse."

I decided to give back what I got. Staring at his crotch I said, "Well, I suppose it's better than having jock itch." He never put me down in that way again.

Sometimes the only antidote to poison is more poison.

• Getting Tough

Getting tough means backing up what you say with action.

It means digging in your heels and fighting for what you decide is right and what you want.

Getting tough means making decisions that are beneficial to you first and that may not be beneficial to anyone else.

Getting tough means stopping other people when they interfere with your plans or hurt your self-esteem. Getting tough is about protecting your own interests and asserting your own values.

Sure, Micki, you say, trample over the world in your selfish, bitchy high heels. But, you know, it's not like that.

Haven't you at least once (only once?) been in this situation: A man you've been absolutely insane about for months finally agrees to forswear all other women. But you know he's cheating. He says he's trying (trying to cheat or trying to stop?), but he keeps staying late at the office with that lovely new supervisor and having long lunches with tennis partners, and you are going out of your mind with jealousy and despair.

As much as you want this man's love, how much are you really getting? What is this relationship that should be smothering you in warm, glowing love really doing to you? You have only to look at your face (like gray parchment) and your eyes (like shriveled raisins from crying and lack of sleep) to see!

So you Get Tough. You tell him that you cannot live with this free-and-easy arrangement. For you it's exclusivity or nothing. And this time you mean it.

There comes a point when you stand by your own values and don't back down; enough is enough.

If he leaves you, he leaves you. It hurts all right, it hurts like hell, but you are no longer putting up with an intolerable situation. You are wounded to the core, but are you any more injured than before you took a stand and stuck to it? What I've learned from my life experience is *never* to hang around to be treated badly.

You have to make the choices that are best for you. Sometimes you have to act before you are acted upon. It's difficult and painful and shocking, but it is the positive, assertive thing to do.

Now let me tell you a well-kept secret. Doing the "right" thing does not—repeat, not—lead to instant happiness and satisfaction. It doesn't "fix" everything that was wrong. It doesn't provide you with instant answers to all your problems. It may be the right thing to do in the circumstances, but don't expect the world to stand up and applaud your actions. You do it for you; you don't need an audience, so don't expect flowers.

Many times I've heard women say, "I don't have the guts to go." Ask yourself: What is it doing to your guts to stay?

Every time you back up what you say with authoritative action, the easier it gets to act again, and the more people will listen to you because they respect you. They will learn that both professionally and personally, when you say something you mean it.

The nice thing about taking action and ending a trauma is that once it's over and you've agonized and had your cry or visit to a psychiatrist or whatever it takes, you can move ahead with your life. A new man, a new job is just around the corner, with a whole new set of problems, to be sure, but once you've solved one . . .

• *Action Defeats Fear*

Don't we all know that's true.

How many job interviews, dates, and responsibilities have you stewed and fussed over only to find that once they actually arrived, once you got on with them, there was nothing to fear?

I used to stew and fret and drive everyone within fifty miles of me berserk before having to make a speech. Once up on the podium, not only did I open my mouth and words came out, but I found I enjoyed it. Action is so much easier on the nerves than anticipation.

Action brings relief in painful, new situations.

When my husband and I separated, I found the first few weekends apart unbearably lonely. The children were with him, and I was by myself in an empty house.

Those weekends stretched before me like an eternal desert until I took action. I called every friend I had—married, single, divorced, widowed, crazy, and sane—and invited them to brunch with one stipulation: Bring a friend. Soon it was sardine time as they came crushing through the door.

It was hectic and mad, but it was fun, too. The house was filled with noise and laughter and bustling activity and new faces—just what I needed.

If a brunch for a crowd big and rowdy enough to fill a football stadium isn't your style (it wasn't mine after the thrill wore off on the fourth weekend), there's still no need to sit alone and stew.

My action scaled down just as my need did. Soon I preferred to ramble around town, going to the art gallery, a museum, or window-shopping, casually exchanging smiles with a few other "regulars" on these weekend strolls. It felt good to have both the freedom of being alone and a little brush with the outside world.

The point is that by doing something—anything—rather than sinking into a sea of loneliness and despair, I kicked off that killer depression.

Any psychologist can tell you that women fall prey to this gray, miserable fog twice as frequently as men. Depression must be nipped in the bud before our whole garden of delights is frosted over. It kills the zest for life, it murders affection and joy, it strangles happiness. It holds you back from relating to others. Fight it with everything you've got, and if you need help fighting it run, don't walk, for help.

My friend Beth got over her post-divorce blues by literally gutting her (it used to be their) house from rafters to basement. She ripped down walls, tore out ceilings, and stripped floors. Now, in addition to feeling fully recovered within, she has a stunningly renovated house.

A neighbor mended her broken heart by taking a three-month sabbatical from work and hopping a plane to Europe where she swept through the male population like the plague of old. Extreme action, but it worked. A more altruistic young woman told me she filled every spare moment working with children with learning disabilities. "The intense concentration and devotion needed to help these kids completely blotted Simon out of my mind," she swears. "I didn't have time to grieve over him or my broken heart."

The message is: Take action. It will help you take heart.

• Intimidation

Intimidation is about power.

The celebrity who snubs you in public, the boss who mentions a cut in pay to demanding workers, the man who casually lets drop that if you don't like sailing, he knows plenty of women who do—they're all practicing the same black art of intimidation. They're all wielding a power that they have only because you give it to them.

Intimidated people are fearful, afraid, and overawed. Sometimes there's good reason to be, like when you spill your drink over the four-hundred-pound ex-wrestler at the bar, and sometimes it's just silliness, like when you weakly allow your hairdresser to "punk" your hair in green and purple stripes.

Sometimes a childish dependency keeps us intimidated, like clinging to a favorite shrink or feeling absolutely lost in the dress department without your favorite saleswoman on hand.

I have felt intimidated in the most ridiculous situations. Recently I was sitting in the hair salon in a spa in Florida. I heard a familiar voice coming from the next chair. Sitting in the same pink robe as everyone else, her hair in curlers and wearing no makeup, was Elizabeth Taylor. I wanted to say something to her, but what could I say to a legend? Why did you gain weight? I liked your performance in *National Velvet*?

I stuttered and spluttered trying to start a conversation, but I opened my mouth and nothing came out. Her power over me was totally self-inflicted. True, she is a fabulously wealthy, world-famous star; but she was just another woman in the salon. In no way did she try to intimidate me; I did it to myself.

On a more serious level, intimidation can ruin a relationship and scar you badly. I know a lovely woman who was in therapy for years after living with a bully who intimidated her emotionally.

Whenever she got too independent (in his eyes), he'd casually mention an interesting new woman at the office. All his little innuendos kept her in her place. She was too afraid to express her real feelings in case they displeased him and he walked out. Her insecurity and the fact that she loved him obsessively was his cue to turn on the intimidation tactics.

Don't let yourself be an intimidated little rabbit who is always knuckling under. Build your self-esteem, set your own parameters, and get in touch. Most intimidators are bullies, and most bullies are cowards. Stand up to them, and they deflate like overblown balloons.

• The Art of Negotiation

If you think negotiating is something that happens between union leaders and management, or lawyers and judges, think again.

Life is one long negotiation, from the time you test your parents to see if it's okay to spit Pablum on the Persian carpet until you make a deal for the bed with the best view in the old folks' home.

Dealing, bargaining, wheeling, negotiating: Whatever you call it, it's going on around you every day.

Herb Cohen, author of *You Can Negotiate Anything* (a must-read), says: "Life is a game and negotiating a way of life." Cohen and I agree that you can get almost anything you want if you are a skillful negotiator, so it's important to try and learn a few tricks.

In a conflict with others you have three options: knuckle under, fight, or negotiate. The third one holds out the most satisfactory resolution for both parties, produces the most winners, and is the path for mature thinkers.

We strike bargains for what we want in life with everyone around us—children, husband, friends, parents, employers—so don't think you're doing something new. You're trying to learn some old tricks better. Yes, your son can have the car if he polishes the windows; yes, you'll go to the football game with your man if he comes to that new movie with you; yes, you'll do that extra project for your harried boss if you can have a long weekend. Recognize it? That's life. That's negotiating. Deal the cards. Let's play.

Women feel guilty even thinking about negotiating. They fear it means being sneaky, underhanded, manipulative, and other "unfeminine" things. But negotiating makes you an effective and assertive person. It puts you on an equal footing with other smart players around you and earns you respect. It will also get you what you want. I had to learn to negotiate fast enough in this business, and it was only after I'd been fleeced a couple of times that I caught on.

Timing is all-important no matter what you're negotiating. Five p.m. is not a good time to ask your boss for a raise. The doorstep of a dinner party is not the time to remind your spouse he promised not to drink and flirt.

Before you can negotiate you need to get the facts, not only about what you want and need, but also about what's involved for the other party.

I was dealing with a smart cookie of a producer about making a fruit juice commercial years ago. They wanted me to be buried, nude, up to my neck in sand! (Are there crazy people in television or what?)

"What's wrong with the idea?" they asked.

"I'm allergic," I lied.

"If you won't do it, you won't get the part."

"I won't do it."

"Harry, she'll look just as good in a bikini in a lounge chair."

We settled on a sun dress on a balcony!

Okay, I "won" that one, but the producer and the client were also happy! They got the face they wanted in a sunny, summery setting drinking their juice; that was all they really wanted underneath their fancy talk.

But I based my negotiating on solid information: I knew the juice company wanted *me* for these commercials. There wouldn't have been time to find a replacement, and we were on location; flying someone else in would have been costly. I used these cards to come up trumps.

Negotiating is not a win-lose situation; it's win-win.

It doesn't mean walking all over your opponents but walking beside them on some issues if they'll come over to your side of the street on others. Be prepared to give up a little yourself, and you will get a lot back.

This means compromise, and for some people the word compromise suggests cop-out. But I believe it keeps the world from being divided into bullies and victims. You don't want to be, and you don't *have* to be, either of those!

IV

Having It All— Is It Possible?

Now that we've talked about negotiating your way to success, you might ask yourself: "What am I negotiating for? What is it I want out of life?"

Of course, if you're like me you'll answer: "Everything"—and why shouldn't you have it all? Yet, just how possible is it? How many pieces of life can you juggle: yourself, a relationship, a career, children?

When I grew up I looked around, and there were very few women who had broken out of the traditional female mold. The only ones who had were movie stars. We all looked to them with a feeling of envy, because through their own abilities they had attained fame, money, power, and prestige—things that were out of the reach of the ordinary woman.

When I interviewed Gloria Swanson, Joan Fontaine, and Kitty Kelly, biographer of Elizabeth Taylor, I was fascinated to hear a similar theme in all their stories. As they worked their way through numerous marriages—four, five, six—each movie star would talk of giving it all up, settling down with a man, and living the fantasy they had always had of "real" happiness: a home with a white picket fence, a man, two kids, and a dog. Talk about destroyed illusions! All the time we were wishing to be in their very glamorous shoes making love to Paul Newman, Stewart Granger, and Richard Burton in technicolor, they, in fact, were looking at those "ordinary" women who they thought had picture-book happiness. You see, they, too, had bought what the culture had to sell—the "happily ever after" fantasy.

Maybe this says it all:

> I envy my girlfriend because she owns
> One man, two kids, a dog, and her own home.
> My girlfriend envies me 'cause I *don't* own
> One man, two kids, a dog, and my own home.

True, isn't it? The housewife looks at the stylish career woman and sees only her freedom, a new car, and winter holidays in Portugal. Looking back at her is the career woman who envies the housewife's warm home, beautiful children, loving mate, and sense of belonging somewhere. Each thinks the other "has it all." Actually, neither one has the whole picture.

In this decade of changes for women, this is what I've seen: very successful career women who have their identity, autonomy, R.R.S.P., and IUD. The one thing they don't have is a date on Saturday night.

I've interviewed displaced homemakers: widowed or divorced women left on their own after a lifetime of raising a family. They gave all of themselves to others, doing what they were "supposed to do," and then felt ripped off and depressed, because they didn't do anything for themselves along the way.

I have seen women trade in one bill of goods for another. When I grew up, a husband was the ultimate answer. He would make me feel secure, complete me, transform me, make me better than I was before. If I didn't have a husband I was a failure as a woman.

Many women of today's generation have substituted the word "career" for the word "husband." And just as a husband can add to your life, not make your life, so too can work not entirely fulfill all your personal needs.

When Leonard and I vacationed at a resort in Northern Ontario we met a New York couple and spent some time with them. The woman was a mystery to me. She was what I'd call New York chic: beautifully dressed, sassy, fast-talking, sharp, and shrewd. But every time she opened her mouth she sounded like small-town gospel community in Kansas!

"Oh, my Arthur," she'd say. "He likes his eggs done just like this," or: "My Arthur, he doesn't like to dance, so we don't go dancing," or: "My Arthur, it's very important his shirts get starched just right."

Finally, eaten alive with curiosity, I asked about her background.

This smart cookie was the former head of a large Manhattan personnel agency, a one-woman success story in the tough, wheeling-and-dealing business world. She was in her mid-forties when she'd met Arthur, and he'd swept her off her Maud Frizon-ed feet. She'd quit her high-flying, fast-paced executive existence and settled down to being Mrs. Arthur in a suburban castle somewhere; she even drove him to the commuter station every morning and picked him up at night.

She swore she didn't regret any of the power and prestige back in Manhattan. "Arthur," she told me, "was the missing piece of my life. I grabbed it."

Going in exactly the opposite direction is Dr. Sonya Friedman, author of *Men Are Just Desserts*. I interviewed her when she was in her mid-forties and enjoying a spectacular career success.

She'd fallen in love for the first time at the age of fourteen and had written her intended a love letter almost every day until they were married. Once she was in that blissful state, he'd told her what to wear, who to see, where to go. A thousand instructions and two children later, she'd pursued her missing piece, too: Back she went to school, graduated as a psychologist, became the host of a popular radio program and cable television show, and was, when I met her, on a national tour to promote her book. In her mid-life success, she could look back and say that she'd had to do it. It was her time. She'd had her family and then needed to do other things.

Two women, totally opposite directions, but both after that missing piece.

If I were the farmer's daughter, I'd never put all my eggs in one basket. I advise you to spread your assets around. Instead of pouring all your energy into one half of your life and shutting off the other, try to keep something for yourself and someone to share it with. I call it my "Somebody-Something" theory. Past experience tells me it's good to have something of your own that gives you a feeling of accomplishment. It's also important to have a caring person to share those accomplishments and yourself with.

One doesn't diminish the other. A relationship and a career demand such different things of you and give back (just as important) such different things. One fills the need to be cherished, loved, and acknowledged as a woman, the other the need to be respected as a person of achievement and self-reliance. Both require energy and commitment, and both add to your sense of well-being and confidence: They just add in different ways. The question is: Does it have to be an either/or situation?

• Career and Love: Do Passionate Pursuits Detract from One Another?

Yes, sometimes, but not always. They don't have to; it can be worked out. Let me explain.

I have seen women who can't operate on two tracks. They are passionately consumed by their work and not prepared to make a deep commitment to a man.

Robyn is like that. She's "in banking" (even her close

friends don't know exactly what this financial wizard does), and her job takes her on the road half the year. She's been away as long as three months at a stretch, and she loves it.

"My job is prestigious," she says. "You don't find many women doing work at this level. I'm not throwing away this chance; Ted just has to understand. He does, but I know it's hard on him."

Does she expect Ted to sit home and watch old movies every Saturday night?

"Of course not. I know he sees friends, sometimes women friends. They have dinner. I don't ask about dessert. I won't necessarily be traveling forever; I just hope when I come up for air, he's still around. He has to know he's number two in my life right now, and if he can live with it, so can I."

Ted is cautious and noncommittal. "I keep telling myself: If I'd been offered a high-powered job like hers, would I have turned it down for her? No."

They are an extreme case, I know, but the heart of their dilemma is at the heart of every working/loving woman's dilemma. With both a man and a manager putting pressure on you, you get squeezed. Who does come first? The answer is *you*. Whatever you need most right now to fulfill yourself is what's right. We all try to give our major commitments equal time, but most of us are lopsided somewhere along the line.

It's not always the man who loses out. Plenty of women I know have turned down promotions that would have meant extended hours, travel, or moving to another city, because they didn't want to jeopardize their relationship. However, one burning passion sometimes causes the other to cool.

I have seen the toughest, most career-minded woman just melt into pools of ineffectiveness over a new man. A friend of mine who worked freelance used to pray every time she started a new job, "Please, God, don't let me fall for anyone now; let me have my mind to myself so I can work." She claimed that her income fluctuated in inverse ratio to her love life. When she was bonkers over a new man, her productivity declined dramatically.

Don't you know that slavery: falling over the filing cabinet every time the phone rings in case it's him (it's always an inquiry from accounting!), or calling the boss by his name accidentally, or not hearing someone who's positively shouting for your attention.

Some crazy people actually work better when they're madly besotted. It gives them bundles of energy and zing, and they sweep through the day's business like a cyclone so they can get home to the night business of love.

Does it ever work out? Can you be a top achiever in the boardroom and the bedroom for life? Two books, *Pathfinders* by Gail Sheehy and *Life Prints* by Grace Baruch, Rosalind Barnett, and Caryl Rivers (must-reads), that deal with the issue of love and work say that women with the highest sense of well-being have both.

That is the happy state of affairs in my life at this time. To maintain it requires communication, trust, and flexibility from both of us. There's always a lot happening when two independent people pursue their individual passions, and it's easy for the most important element, the relationship, to get crowded out. I think it is key that each partner, no matter how dedicated to their career, reaffirm the importance of the other in their life, not only by words and actions, but also by a conscious commitment of time and energy to the relationship. It's the only way to keep the romance alive and in so doing keep the relationship alive. Each couple has to work out their own life formulas based on ego strengths, needs for security, and internal and external demands. It can be done effectively if there is a strong mutual commitment and if both parties are willing to make compromises. The benefits of pursuing both your passions are worth every bit of the effort.

• *Two out of Three Ain't Bad*

For most women there are three major pieces to life's jigsaw puzzle: love, work, and family. To find those pieces and fit them together is not simple. It involves timing, intensity, and balance.

Let me explain: I have found that there are ages and stages. For some women their twenties are devoted to marriage and child-rearing; suddenly, in their thirties, they plunge into a career when their marriages are comfortably settled and their children on their feet.

Toddy, aged thirty-nine and mother of five, just completed her MBA after five years of part-time study. A group of us (her cronies) threw a surprise graduation party. We rented caps and gowns, and in her laundry room we presented her with a calculator wrapped in a disposable diaper to celebrate her hard-earned achievements on both fronts.

It works equally in reverse—women who have spent their twenties locked in heartfelt commitment to their jobs are suddenly, in their thirties, casting around for a man to settle down with and longing for a baby. One close girlfriend, Hanna, a stockbroker, is a first-time mother at thirty-seven. She used to talk incessantly (and often, to me, incomprehensibly) about debentures and treasury notes. Now she chortles with the same conviction about diapers and feeding schedules.

These are two familiar scenarios. There are dozens more as women juggle the pieces, trying to fit them together. It takes years to cultivate your talents and skills and years to build a loving relationship and raise a family. And the pressure is on women to do both in the first half of their adult lives. Consequently, there is a continual struggle between intensity and balance. To achieve professional excellence—to make it to the upper echelons of the corporate world, to get your name in lights, or to build your own thriving business—requires fierce dedication. Something's got to give.

A good friend of mine in her late thirties is an executive at a top American television network. Whenever I visit her (having gone through five secretaries just to get near her inner sanctum) she says with a grin, "Micki, I have to pinch myself to believe I'm here. I've come so far, it's still like a dream." Then she confides, "But you know, what I want more than anything in the world now is a baby. At this point in my career it's impossible for me to stop and have one, yet on the other hand time is running out, so it's impossible for me not to."

When I interviewed Judy Chicago, the artist who created the revolutionary feminist work of art, *The Dinner Party*, she told me emphatically that people should stop telling women that they can "have it all easily," because for most of us there are difficult and demanding choices to be made.

Sometimes you make these choices yourself ... sometimes fate does it for you. Betty's husband died suddenly at the age of thirty-eight, leaving her with four children and no insurance. Betty, a homemaker and closet writer until that time, suddenly had to scramble. Today she is a well-known writer selling articles to magazines, newspapers, and television and has written a best-seller.

Brenda, an award-winning journalist with a major newspaper, fell in love with an internationally known lawyer when she interviewed him for a story. To be with him she moved to another city. "The timing for my career wasn't right," she said, "but I knew he was. I took three steps backward in my career to follow my man, but I took one gigantic step forward in my personal life."

Timing was a crucial element for Brenda and for Patty. She ran a small but successful chocolate chip cookie business from her kitchen, supplying gourmet shops and restaurants. Last time I saw her, she had closed up shop. "Why?" I asked. "I had to make a critical business decision. I had to expand, buy a factory, sell to grocery chains. But with three kids under the age of ten and no financial pressure, I felt the timing wasn't right. I couldn't, in good conscience, make that commitment of time and energy." "What about the missed opportunity?" I inquired. "I'll create another one a few years down the line." Industrious woman, clever mind: No doubt she will.

There are turning points in every woman's life, but no one can tell you when yours are. You'll know, because what has been consuming you for ten years is suddenly flat and uninteresting and lonely: You need something more. Today each individual woman is on her own timetable. At this time you may have part of what you want, but life will come up with new opportunities, scenarios, and fresh beginnings. Life is full of options and choices—to have it all you have to plan for it, integrate it, and grab your chance when it comes around. I like to think of life as a soap opera: Just when you think you've got everything in place, fate throws some new twist, and what was an important priority is all up in the air again. Be grateful for that. Every new chapter in life brings new opportunities, something that you can learn to use to your advantage.

In my life there has been a constant struggle between intensity and balance. As I've moved into the different stages of my life, the focus of my intensity has shifted. When I was first married my relationship and my career were what I lived for. Then when Lance and Lisa came along, even though I still worked freelance, acting and writing, the children took up the biggest part of my life. As anyone with two babies two years apart can tell you, my relationship and career slipped to second and third place. When my marriage ended and the children were a bit older and a bit more independent (thank goodness!), I was free to throw a different kind of energy into my career. For a number of years, it was kids and career. Now things have turned around again: My children are young adults on their own, and my relationship with a special man is ultra-important. The thrust of my energy and interest is relationship-career again.

So I *have* had it all—relationship, kids, career—

although the order and intensity kept changing. This is Micki's "Two-out-of-Three" theory, and it's not bad.

● *Three out of Three: Hello, Superwoman!*

Hello, Superwoman! How do you leap from the office to the kitchen to the nursery in one fell swoop without snagging your pantyhose? Plenty of women are doing it: trying to be perfect employees, perfect mothers, and perfect wives. If guilt or stress don't get you, exhaustion will. What is the best way to cope? Betty Friedan said, "Lower your standards." Standards for perfection in business were set by generations of men who had full-time wives helping them at home, and standards of housework were set by generations of women who defined their whole existence through housekeeping. Personal standards that are unrealistically high can be a woman's own worst enemy. It's time to call for redefinitions, and it's very important that those redefinitions be clear in your own mind.

What does motherhood mean to you? What does marriage mean? Or career success? Elizabeth Barrett Browning wrote: "How do I love thee? Let me count the ways ..." If the ways are measured by how many clean socks are in the drawer, how polished the kitchen floor is, or how many pot roasts you cook, there might be trouble. If it's measured by the quality of time, not the quantity, by the emotional support you offer your family and by the depth of sharing, then there's a strong possibility that your marriage, family, and you will come through intact. Unfortunately, we still haven't got rid of images of who men and women are and what they are supposed to be to each other.

For example, the new, sympathetic man is concerned about his working wife and talks a good line about helping out around the house, but he often doesn't lift a proverbial finger. A recent three-year study examining fourteen hundred dual-career marriages shows that the working wife spends an average of twenty-six hours a week on housework. Her husband spends thirty-six minutes. As my girlfriend Barbara says, "Bob carries a dish from the table to the sink and then stands there expecting a medal." In families with children under age eleven, only one father in five helped out with the youngsters.

Sex becomes as much of a hassle as housework. Women, so deeply fatigued from doing two jobs, said they had little zest left for sex. Lust and dust, it seems, are incompatible!

So what are you to do? Delegate! But to whom? Everyone in your family. (Barbara Woodhouse told me her dog did the vacuuming!) Make a list. Instead of telling them what to do, let them pick out the chores that they want to be responsible for. If they don't do their end, you don't do yours.

Don't do it! Buy permanent press clothes, have the groceries delivered, and send the sheets to the laundry.

Hire someone! The first extra money I made, I spent on a cleaning woman. To me this wasn't a luxury; it was a necessity. I considered it an investment in my most important asset: me. "Are you kidding, Micki?" you ask. "I can't afford that." Neither could I when I first started out, but then I started thinking like a businesswoman: You have to spend money to make money. Men rarely think of functioning without a secretary or some sort of back-up staff, yet women somehow think they must do everything themselves, no matter how busy their schedules. I've never had the cleanest house in town, but I've had one heck of an interesting life!!!

Learn to say "No" guilt-free. Just as you need to "let up and let go" around the house, the same applies to work and bringing up children. A report doesn't need to be rewritten four times. Kids can make their own lunches—you don't need to do it. Every woman has to come to terms with her own nature and philosophy when it comes to raising children. Personally, I could never stay home all the time, even when my kids were babies. If I was home all day I got scratchy and irritable, and so did the kids. But when I was working I was up and excited and brimming with energy, and they picked that up.

Probably the most difficult and challenging thing I've had to do in my life was raise two children. Jobs come and go, but children are forever. You have to face them and see how they turn out. Mine have been a powerful bond in my life, binding me to something bigger and better than the day's immediate triumphs and disasters. I feel I have given my kids roots and wings: roots to provide a solid base throughout life and wings to fly.

• Shifting Priorities: Maybe That's What You Wanted Five Years Ago

It's wonderful to care passionately and totally for whatever turns you on today—but why assume you'll still be lit up over it in five or ten years' time? The things you want now you may no longer want then, or they may no longer want you. Jobs change, men come and go, and children grow up. Priorities, like the ground under your feet, shift!

How I wanted my own television show! It gave me recognition, money, prestige, and feedback. But after six years the thing I loved and wanted was wearing me out. What you want and crave so desperately can turn on you, and you have to know when to give it up. When the challenge, fun, excitement of anything is over, it's time to move on. That's one talent I've always had. I'm not a tumbleweed, but I've always picked up and moved on to something else (usually better) when the sparkle wore off and I had given it my all. I didn't grind to a halt because I reached a certain age or stage. I shifted gears and moved on.

Marlo Thomas is a great example of a woman faced with shifting priorities. For years this outspoken feminist couldn't see a place for marriage in her get-ahead life.

"I used to think of marriage as a giant vacuum cleaner

that sucked out your brains," she said.

Her career was her life, her reason to get out of bed in the morning.

"All the career appointments on my calendar were written in ink," said Marlo, "and the personal ones in pencil. Those could change or go anytime."

Now, in addition to pursuing a career, Marlo is Mrs. Phil Donahue, and her priorities have done an about-face. And so have the calendar appointments. It's the professional ones that now get the easy-to-erase treatment.

On one show I interviewed six women about their choice of whether to go back to work after having a baby or stay home. The three high-powered career women who had been quite emphatic about their quick return to work after pregnancy were the three who ended up staying at home once they came face-to-face with their own little bundles of reality. The three homemakers who had held part-time jobs on and off and felt they would definitely remain at home were the ones who returned to the work force as soon as possible. Sometimes changes in your life are made when nature and necessity demand it.

At different times in your life, one priority rises in ascendancy—revel in its importance and impact but, just like the new mothers, don't be surprised if one day something else takes up a lot of your energy and heart. In fact, count on it, because the eighteen-year-old you cannot fully predict what the thirty-five-year-old you will need—and who, at thirty-five, knows what her life will be like at fifty? Which brings us to a very important question ...

• What Really Makes You Happy?

Whatever you choose to do in life, whatever your goals or driving desires, they should be tailored to what you want, what makes you happy. This is the purpose of everything in this book: to build up confidence and self-esteem and desire better things in life, like career satisfaction and loving relationships. It's all to make a happier you. It doesn't matter what magazines and movies say should make you happy or what thrills your best friend: This is for you.

The fashionable (that doesn't mean right) emphasis today is on career. A woman I know told me a very revealing story. When people asked her what she did, she answered truthfully: "I'm a housewife and mother of six." Their eyes would glaze over, and they would edge away, treating her as if she was a nobody.

So she changed her story: "I used to work, but when my best friend died, I adopted her six children and now look after them full-time." The crowd would gather, fascinated, intrigued by her new "career." Funny how raising your own children isn't considered work, but raising someone else's is!

Like the woman in this story, none of us are immune from society's pressures. Therefore, I think it's increasingly important to strip away the myths and misconceptions about women and the way they live, especially for women making nontraditional choices. Conclusive research, as published in the book *Life Prints*, brought out these facts: A woman who works hard at a challenging job is doing something positive for her mental health; marriage and children do not guarantee well-being; the lack of a husband and children does not guarantee misery; doing and achieving are at least as important to a woman's self-esteem as relationships and feelings. In the last two decades the options for women have increased dramatically: remaining childless, choosing to be a parent by oneself, choosing serial monogamy, staying single by choice, and making a career a life commitment, shooting for the top. Yet what is possible for this generation is still hard to swallow for the previous one. As my friend Robyn told me somewhat ruefully, "Not only did my mother keep sending me anniversary presents four years after the divorce, but she never mentioned my separation to friends and relatives—then I turned up at a family wedding with my new boyfriend."

One of the pitfalls that often trips women up is thinking that a Big Change—abandoning career, changing jobs, setting up house with a new man, having a baby on their own—will bring instant happiness. Changes don't do this. They bring a new set of problems and adjustments along with the joys and rewards.

So before you have "N.W." (New Woman) tattooed on your right thigh, consider this story. A pregnant woman in her mid-twenties approached me after a speech I had given on dual-career marriages in which I had described my own life in terms of my "Two-out-of-Three" theory. She told me she was a physiotherapist working full-time with a twenty-two-month-old at home. "I'm trying to have it all," she sighed, "but I'm not happy. I'm exhausted. I feel like an overstretched elastic band. It felt so good to hear someone say out loud that it's okay to let go of one of the pieces for a while."

Here's a big truth: You don't have to feel guilty if you choose to give something up and let go of one of the pieces. Only you can define your own timetable and stress limits.

Some women handle stress better than others; some handle business stress better than personal stress. My girlfriend Susan, who is an advertising executive, says, "Handling six major accounts is a piece of cake compared to the wear and tear on my nerves of my two toddlers." It isn't easy juggling home and business; they are so dramatically different. Believe me, I know. In business you have to be cool, efficient, and tough; time is money. At home you have to be warm, available, and understanding; time is simply time that is needed to help and heal and feel. Switching on and off between those two roles is something of a schizophrenic act. What's more important? I used to question myself. Preparing for a big television show the next day or helping my kid make a Halloween costume when he insists he wants to go as a tube of Preparation H—talk about priorities!

A recent study of women in their forties and fifties showed that the ones with the highest level of well-being were those who had made commitments to marriage, career, and motherhood before they were out of their twenties. These women weren't driven by the "I gotta be Number One" philosophy. They had reached their aspired career goal along the way and had kept the rest of their life in balance. A lot of young women are postponing marriage and motherhood in pursuit of their career goals, putting off major personal commitments, leaving their options open. The only danger of postponement is that the years slip by. If you forget to integrate some of the other pieces into your life plan, you might outsmart yourself. Statistically it's harder to find a mate as you get older (if you're looking). And, of course, that old biological clock keeps ticking away.

Recently I was talking to one of the most successful broadcasters in this country, a woman in her late thirties. Outwardly she has everything any career woman would envy, but what I saw was one tired lady. We talked about it. "Micki," she said, "I've traveled the world, I have a lot of money, I have everything, but I don't have time to form a relationship with anyone except airline clerks. I can't even think about having children, and my time is running out. I have to reassess what success is about, because if this is it—a lot of exhaustion and lonely nights—I'm not sure I want it any longer. All this used to make me happy; I guess it doesn't anymore."

Change hit Marla, on the other hand, like a Mack truck going sixty miles an hour, and happiness arrived at her doorstep by a very circuitous route. "My husband made a surprise exit. He came with a van over the weekend when I was out of town and took everything but our Billie Holliday records and the laundry hamper. I was a total wreck—wiped out emotionally and financially. The divorce was the most painful experience of my life. I know this sounds crazy, but it was also the best thing that ever happened to me. I was forced to draw on inner strength I never knew I had. I accomplished things I didn't think were possible. I used to dabble in selling cosmetics door-to-door; now, four years later, I'm a top regional supervisor. If anyone had told me where I would be today, and how happy, I wouldn't have believed them."

So what is the magic formula for success and happiness? Each individual woman has to determine her own. You are in the driver's seat, deciding which of life's lanes you will travel in. You deserve the best life has to offer. Pack up your courage and conviction and go after it.

V

Don't Talk About It, Do It!

• *Stop Putting Your Life on Hold*

You know how hard you grit your teeth in an elevator when someone presses the "Hold" button and you sit there steaming (politely), suspended in the elevator shaft, going neither up nor down, while the furniture, twins in strollers, or oil paintings are loaded on. Some women, I fear, spend their entire lives in a holding pattern.

They are the ones who started off so nicely on a solid rise to the top. Good university, nice man, happy marriage, sweet baby—then hold.

Or, in-on-the-ground-floor careerists, they make an impressive rise through company ranks, then options peter out, loose ends abound—and suddenly hold.

There they stay, running on the spot, not moving forward or falling backward.

The years that pass are the years they were supposed to take singing lessons or become company president or open their own business or take a trip around the world. But no dreams come true when life is on hold.

What happens?

Maybe they lose courage or get distracted with other interests. But often they just forget they meant to do something more with their lives. They follow the script and become a wife and mother and forget they could also be an architect or an actress or an entrepreneur. They make a list of all the things their husband, children, and friends need and put their needs at the bottom.

This holding pattern was waved in front of me like a tattered flag after a war by a woman listening to me speak on the secrets of success.

She was a striking, well-dressed woman; we shared coffee after the talk. Her husband, she told me, had died a few years before, the kids had grown up, and she was left with . . . herself. A virtual stranger.

"My kids are out living their own lives," she confided. "I did everything I was supposed to do. I was a good wife and a good mother, but what I did was put my life on hold." She hadn't done anything strictly for herself in twenty-five years. Her body was in the 1980s, she said, but her mind and psyche were languishing in the 1950s.

She had once planned for a career in art and had even taken some design and illustration courses, but then the kids came along, and the family needed her, and the house wanted looking after, and there was the home and school association—so really, who had the time to pursue a dream?

It could wait. Or so she thought. But on that day we sat drinking muddy coffee together, she woke up to find years and opportunities lost forever, days and years that won't come around again.

This is it. *Your life.* Spend it wisely. And that means not putting everything you want to be into a holding pattern and letting it stay there while the world turns. While the people around you grow and change and develop, don't you sit there like a fossil frozen in a prehistoric ice flow! I've seen too many women petrified like rocks!

So why do women put their lives on hold to such a destructive degree?

Sylvia, a charming forty-eight-year-old homemaker, sums it up: "I was afraid to try anything as daring as opening my own business as I'd always dreamed of doing. We didn't really need the money (don't worry, Sylvia, most new businesses lose a fortune at the beginning!), and the kids were settled into a nice home life. I didn't want to disrupt that. I guess I was frightened of changing things, upsetting everyone, causing trouble."

Right, Sylvia. Only "selfish" women upset their loved ones and fail to keep everyone happy and contented as a field full of cows. (Isn't this that "compassion trap" again?)

"Hold" is a safe place.

Life is a place of challenges and risks and excitement and some failures and hurt, too. But such rewards!

Actress Dyan Cannon, who is directing her first film, was asked if she felt nervous about venturing into new territory. After all, she could stay "on hold" as an actress forever.

"I'm terrified," Dyan admits. "I'm scared, but then I've been scared about every single thing I've done in my life, so what's new?"

When fellow actress Joanne Woodward was asked about the personal and creative risks she'd taken, she replied, "To tell the truth, I am an absolute coward. I think I take enormous risks to overcompensate."

Every time I attempt something new or step in a different direction, I'm terrified. The insides of my knees are raw from knocking together. But what I often do is put on my jogging shoes, run around the park, and repeat, "Yes I can, yes I can, yes I can" in time to my running. This way I work off my fear and rekindle my confidence.

There's a great deal of satisfaction in getting to the other side, going through the exercise, attempting, growing. Sometimes it's a disaster, sometimes it's not such a disaster, and sometimes it's great. I learned everything I can do today by going out there and doing it—no holding back.

Women find it easy to put their lives on hold, because society gives them a great big helping hand. Be a nurturer, look after others: That's your role. I have seen women who would never speak up for themselves turn tiger in defense of their families. Support your husband, let your children rise to their full potential, but what about your potential? When will your time come? Later, women say, later.

Later is often too late! You live now—so live.

• *Whatever Happened to Your Dreams?*

Dawn asked herself that question. She was a woman who felt she had been "holding" for too long and was revving up to change all.

"I want to do something, but I don't know what," she said. "I've wasted years of my life—no, not wasted, because my family is happy and secure—but I've wasted myself. I don't even know how to start living for me."

"What do you regret about the years that have passed?" I asked her. "What did you miss out on?"

"Oh, Micki, I don't know if I would have done anything, really, but I always dreamed of playing the piano. We had one when I was a kid, and I never did keep up my music lessons, and I love music, and . . ."

"WAIT," I interrupted. "That's the key word."

"Music?"

"NO."

"Piano?"

"NO! Dream. It's what you've dreamed of doing, it's your dream that you want to make come true."

"But it's just a dream . . ." Dawn began.

"A dream," I said emphatically, "is never 'just a.' A dream is a message, a signal, an inspiration to you. It's a clue to what you really want."

I mean, does anybody dream of scrubbing floors or changing diapers or making meat loaf?

Dawn took the hint, and so should you. She started piano lessons again and last year bought a second-hand piano. This year she's buying a Steinway. She's busy recapturing a little piece of what she's missed, and she's moved off "hold" for life.

What would your dreams tell you?

There is a message in the fluffiest daydream. When I was a teenager, I fantasized about being an actress, a trapeze artist, an opera singer, a ballerina. Today I haven't become all those things. (Me on a trapeze? Not even for a chance to wear those spangled tights.)

But what were my dreams really telling me? That I wanted to perform, that I wanted to do something creative. That's the message I picked up and followed. My daydreams often ended with me being interviewed by a reporter. Was that egotism? Maybe, but I think they were telling me, loud and clear, that I craved recognition for whatever talent I had.

For years I didn't pay attention to my dreams. What about you? Have you been ignoring the messages your dreams are giving you? Lives may go on hold, but dreams don't.

I have heard women say over and over again, "I don't know what I want to do." "Read your dreams," advised a psychologist on my show, "and play the childhood game of 'What if . . .' "

What if I were an Olympic athlete?

What if I were a brain surgeon?

What if I were an actress and won an Oscar?

What if I were a political hostess with Washington and London at my feet?

What if . . . There's no limit. Go on, dream.

Thoreau said, "Thought is a sculptor who can create the person you want to be." He should know. Like many creative people, he got ideas and inspiration from his own dreams and visions.

Dreams can solve problems. The answers just come "in a flash" when you're replaying the scenario in your head.

They help you prepare for the future by guiding you along paths that appeal to you; they ward off boredom and tension and dissipate anger and deep depression.

In that way they are a safety valve.

Dreams can spur on success. Athletes and actors imagine themselves at the finish line or center stage, thereby working out some of the problems in their daydreams before being tested by reality.

Dreams will tell you what kind of person you are. Trust them. They are you. They're telling you what you want, who you are, what you need to be truly fulfilled. Dream on.

• What's Holding You Back?

Take a deep breath and sharpen your pencil. Then check off your favorite excuses.

I am going to do something with my life:

- As soon as the kids are in school.
- As soon as I lose ten pounds.
- As soon as the kids are out of school.
- As soon as something turns up.
- As soon as I lose the ten pounds I gained back.

I would have done it earlier, but:

- I'm too old; I don't have any experience.
- I'm too young; I don't have any experience.
- There are fifty people out there who can do the job better than I can.
- I lost the weight again, and now my thighs are flabby.
- I tried it once, and it didn't work out.
- I don't have a university degree.
- I have a university degree, but everyone knows grads can't get jobs.
- My parents never prepared me for anything, because they didn't think it was important.
- I don't want to upset my husband/kids/mother-in-law.
- I don't need the money, my husband makes enough.
- It's karma: When it'll happen, it'll happen.

• I firmed up my thighs, so I'll do it as soon as I get my nose fixed.

To break the excuse barrier, you need courage.

Wayne Dyer, a psychologist who was a frequent guest on my show, defined courage as "flying in the face of criticism, relying on yourself, being willing to learn from the consequences of all your choices."

He added, especially for women "on hold," that progress and growth are impossible if you do things the way you've always done them.

Crashing through the excuse barrier is anxiety-causing. But good things can come from anxiety: It primes you, makes you stay on your toes, tones up flabby ambition. Excuses prevent you from moving ahead, so tear up your list.

• *There Is No Failure, Only Experience to Grow From*

Okay, now picture this: I am offered a commercial (for hair color, or floor wax, or Chevrolets—what does it matter?) on the condition that I can ride a horse.

Me? A horse? Of course I can ride a horse, I tell them. All you do is put one leg over the side and sit there.

Needless to say, the largest pet I've ever owned is a budgie. I know nothing about horses. Do they sit like camels so you can get on their backs even in high heels, or do you spring into the saddle like the Cisco Kid?

Anyway, the production crew was all set to shoot this commercial in a farmer's field.

The horse was on a hill. I was to ride down the hill, smiling and waving at the camera off across the field.

From a distance, the horse looked manageable. Up close he might as well have been an angry bull elephant.

"Big, isn't it?" I said to the owner.

"Get on, Micki," yelled the director from the field.

Right. Where's the door? Or the steps?

The farmer who owned Old Paint took pity.

He held the "stirrup." (See how much I learned?) I put one foot in and grabbed the horse's fur (sorry, mane) while a farmhand pushed on my bottom with both hands (were both hands really necessary?) and catapulted me into the seat (sorry, that's saddle).

A cinch!

Unfortunately the horse started to move.

And move. And move. Down the hill he galloped with me bumping around frozen in panic on his back. Help!

"Stop!" I screeched, when panic let me unlock my jaw.

He did. Stopped dead, in fact, right in front of the director, who had a bottle of smelling salts under his nose at this point, and pitched me head first into his lap!

"I thought you said you could ride a horse," he gasped.

"I can, but not this one," I told him.

I can see myself there crumpled up, head spinning, covered in sweat and dirt, the butt of uproarious laughter from the crew and contempt from the farmer (to say nothing of the horse).

Would you call this a failure?

Not me. Because they got enough film from that panic-spurred run down the hill to keep me in the commercial (a success!) and I learned something W. C. Fields knew long ago—never work with animals!

If you substitute the word "experience" for "failure" in life, a wealth of richness and endeavor is released. If everything worked out perfectly, smoothly, effortlessly all through life, how boring and incomplete we'd be.

One of the most valuable things I've learned about "failures" is that their lifespan is thirty seconds in the eyes of others and thirty years (if you let them be) in yours. People notice your failures for the length of time it takes to swallow an hors d'oeuvre. You make them an all-day buffet.

Sir Laurence Olivier, perhaps the greatest actor of this century, was once fired from his job as director of the National Theatre in England. (How much more did he have to prove?)

Winston Churchill couldn't get reelected after steering his country through the Second World War.

Babe Ruth, considered by many to be the greatest athlete of all time, set the record for the number of home runs; he also holds the record for the most strikeouts.

Future Oscar winner Katherine Hepburn was carved up in an early review by Dorothy Parker with the immortal line, "Miss Hepburn runs the gamut of emotions from A to B."

A top publisher in this country has to live with the fact that she turned down the manuscript of what went on to be one of the hottest-selling books of the decade. "Well, we're all entitled to one giant blooper, and that's mine," she says philosophically.

I have been told by radio producers to stick to television, by television producers to stick to radio, and by a network executive to get out of both and stay home. And you are agonizing because you got the figures muddled at a sales meeting or couldn't hold together a relationship that had more holes in it than the Titanic!

It's not easy to convince yourself that mistakes aren't hanging offenses, but I've drawn up a list of suggestions that might make it easier for you to drop the word "failure" and go for the word "experience."

• Dissect setbacks with an eye to recharting your path. At what point exactly did things start to go wrong? Then replot the whole scene, casting yourself as the winner. Next time you're faced with a similar situation you'll know how to act.

• Stop blaming it all on "bad luck." You make your

own luck. A wicked fairy isn't out there waiting to trip you up. That's a cop-out. (A good one, though; I've used it myself in weak moments.) I firmly believe that "luck is the residue of design."

• Add persistence to your arsenal. Stick to your goals, even if you have to change the approach and timing. Now that it's an "experience" and not a "failure," it won't derail you.

• Have a good laugh. My bloopers are recorded on video tape which the crew spliced together and presented to me at Christmas. Now I entertain my friends with all my mistakes.

• The Best Chance of Getting What You Want Is Knowing What It Is

Remember high school geometry—the shortest distance between two points is a straight line? Well, it's still true.

The shortest distance between you and your goal of being a prima ballerina/photographer/mother of triplets/corporate bigwig is a clear, straight path uncluttered by guilt, pressure, half-heartedness, exhaustion, insecurity, or indecision.

I see the half-heartedness of people like Maryon who is dying to pick up her career as a fashion coordinator again but feels so torn about leaving her baby, and will her husband survive her long hours, and, oh dear, what should she do?

Or Deirdre, who is dying to quit her job as a political research assistant and get out of the city with her man and set up a little sheep farm and have ten babies (well, maybe eight or nine), but what if she really, really misses the big city and her friends and dies of boredom with all those sheep?

As long as they dither and put off and make weak little stabs at bits of both, nothing will feel good, right, or satisfying. So how do you get your shoes clicking on the yellow brick road to your goal?

Well, believe it or not, the first and sometimes most difficult thing is to decide what you really want.

"Being rich" isn't a goal; neither is "being famous" or "getting married." Flesh out your goals in technicolor! How else will you recognize the bits and pieces of them along the way? Let's have some details.

Fame as what? A painter? What kind of painter? Oils? Watercolors? What subjects would you paint? What size canvasses would you work on? Who would be your inspiration? Who would be your customers? What galleries in town would most likely take your style of work?

A man? How tall is he? What color are his eyes? How does he earn his daily bread? Is he gentle, or does he prefer to roughhouse? Would he want children? Would you? Does he like dogs? What will you buy him for your first anniversary? Deep down inside you know. Say it!

Fuzzy, undefined goals are for dreamers. That's okay if the dreaming leads you somewhere. Details are for the dreamers who turn into doers.

Riches? How will you get the money? Through your job? What career? What university will you attend? What will you specialize in? Do you know of firms handling accounts that might interest you? How many weekends and holidays are you willing to give up to work? Does this mean no marriage or family for at least ten years?

Plan it out. Goals involve all the pieces of your life and personality. They should fit together comfortably if it's going to work.

Lynn Tribbling, a dynamic Toronto social scientist who frequently guested on my show, says that the laws of success can be learned and are instrumental in forming a plan to reach your goals. They work for both your personal life and your career. She calls them her ABCs. A is for awareness: awareness of your abilities and a realistic assessment of them. B is for the burning desire, the motivation to keep you going. C is for concrete goals. D is for a definite plan. E is for the effort: the perseverance and discipline needed to go after those goals. And F is for a friend, someone to give you moral support and encouragement.

Make a list if it helps; draw diagrams with arrows pointing sideways, down, and up, up, up. Look at the lists and diagrams every night before falling asleep until you know your goal plan the way you know your address and telephone number.

And have faith: Believe it can be done.

The Duke of Wellington, asked by his anxious generals and commanders on the day of the Battle of Waterloo what his plans were, replied simply: "To beat the French." Now that is clear-sightedness in setting a goal!

While you're creating your game plan for success, don't feel you have to be bound by tradition. A new idea or fresh approach, even if it sounds outlandish, can open doors along the way.

I once had (I thought) a brilliant idea for a TV series on life-and-death situations called "Life on the Line."

I tried phone calls and letters, but I couldn't get one producer to give me the time of day. So I attacked with originality. I sent little black coffins with tiny nooses inside and my name and number to key producers. Three called back in one afternoon. I never did sell the idea, but I did get their attention, they did listen, and I made some useful contacts for the next brilliant idea. Don't get hung up doing things the right way. What right way?

A very important point: Never think you're the best today that you can ever be. Tomorrow you could be better! Every day you're alive is a day to improve, to learn, to polish an old skill or pick up a new one. (I had a friend in college who said this about men.)

Don't ever become complacent. Any performer can tell you that being comfortable, accepting, and complacent is death to creativity, energy—and success.

• Get the Action Habit

All the dreams and plans in the galaxy are useless if

they live in your handkerchief drawer until a grand-daughter unearths them along with dried-up sprigs of lavender and old bars of scented soap!

That's not what they're for. Don't save them. They are for now. And that means getting the action habit, because it will turn a dream into reality.

I know a woman who runs a course on how to start your own business. She tells this story:

"I started out in one of my first classes with about forty women. They were all crazy to start their own business. Week by week, fewer and fewer women came to the class. I couldn't understand it. I was piling on the information, telling them about financing, bank loans, interest rates, searching out store space, buying merchandise—all vital information. Finally, when the class dwindled down to ten people, I screwed up my courage and asked one of the remaining women why the others had dropped out.

" 'Because,' she said, 'it's easier to dream.' "

These women had dreamed of opening their own business, but the idea of putting the dream into action with all the hard work, effort, risk, and responsibility had scared them off. They had run back to their warm little hutches and left the real action to someone else.

It's a shame, because it means that gallons of potential and satisfaction and rewards are just poured down the drain.

Dreams are comforting. Work is hard.

The action habit means planting seeds in order to make things happen. Before getting my own talk show, I used to drop by the station every couple of months to keep my face fresh in the producers' minds. Nothing happened immediately (how's three years?), but when a slot for a new show opened up, they thought of me. Finally the seeds had sprouted. One mustache and three interviews later, they began to bloom. I've come to the conclusion that there is a Micki's Law operating in the universe: *If you plant enough seeds and tend them, eventually something will grow.*

Think of yourself as a big, beautiful Rolls Royce, shining, gleaming, polished, envied. And empty. No gas. You ain't going nowhere. (Oh, all right, you can be a little, sleek, chic sports car.)

Without the gas, no matter how good you think you are, you're standing still, hidden on a back street. Motivation is the gas, the fuel, the burning desire. Call it what you will, but call it!

A woman who plays tennis at my club got divorced three years ago and was determined to marry again and marry rich. She hungered. She became a yacht broker to meet her mate, and it worked. Now that's motivation!

A married man who fell head over heels (tête over pieds?) in love with a gorgeous French woman learned her language in four months, divorced his wife, and married her. His passion drove him to language school! That's motivation.

Desire can motivate, but so can need. When I asked the editor of a top national magazine what the key to her success was, she said, "My husband left me with two children and twelve dollars in the bank."

Motivation is what keeps you moving, what gnaws at you to get out there and go for it.

A few years back I had a very important meeting to go to with Alan Thicke, recently of talk show fame but in those days a network television producer. He was looking for comedy writers, and I thought, well, hey, I know a few jokes. . . . Besides, I needed a job.

The morning of the interview I was playing tennis in a tournament fifty miles north of the city. No problem, I thought. I'll be back in plenty of time to get gorgeous and make the meeting.

Of course fate was lying in wait for me. I went to the tournament in a girlfriend's car; she locked her keys inside; I was fifty miles from a bath, and my interview was getting closer.

Do not despair, Micki, I kept telling myself, you will

get to that interview if you have to jog all the way!

I didn't jog; instead, I hitched a lift on the first vehicle that came along—a cattle truck. I climbed in among the cows and hay and *odeur de barn* and rode the fifty miles back to town. The driver dropped me near a girlfriend's house.

"You always said you'd give me the shirt off your back," I said as she stood and stared open-mouthed at my tennis "grays" and straw-covered body. "So give me the shirt off your back."

She did. I didn't have time to wash. I leaped into her car, drove like a madwoman, and made the interview with seconds to spare. I couldn't look that bad, I figured: I'd wiped the straw off my legs and dumped a vial of Chanel No. 5 down my cleavage.

I must have been okay, because Thicke hired me. Maybe he was impressed by my determination, because he didn't even mention the clump of cow dung stuck to my shoe or the odd combination of silk shirt and smelly tennis shoes. Nice man.

If you want something badly enough, you'll find a way.

Motivation also separates needs from wants. We all need food and shelter. We don't need Giorgio Armani or Chateau Lafite Rothschild or three weeks at a spa, but some of us want them. The question is: How badly? What are you willing to do to get your share of them? That's the seed of motivation.

You may lust after a career so badly you'll give up a comfortable life and spend four penurious years as a student to get the skills you need.

Billions of actresses take parts in low-budget horror films and bathroom tissue commercials in the hopes that these will not only pay the rent but also lead to something bigger and better. (If only Robert Altman had seen me on that horse.)

Women are driven to starve themselves so they can be the next Christie Brinkley look-alike cover girl. Women are motivated to learn sailing, fly fishing, mountain climbing, and sheepshearing so they can get that man!

Sometimes motivation is profitable in the millions.

I saw a fascinating show on television about self-made millionaires. One woman who couldn't find any cosmetics she liked made her own from fruit and vegetables and founded an all-natural cosmetics empire.

A former hippie couldn't find the herbal teas he liked to drink in North America and founded a multi-million-dollar tea business.

A housewife who wanted to lose weight started a neighborhood exercise class in her basement. Today she owns a chain of exercise studios across the country and has made a record and written a book.

These self-made whizzes were motivated by their desire to do something better than it was already being done, to fill a gap, to create something themselves, to put their dreams into action.

If you can't find what you want out there, maybe it's time to create it yourself.

Get going!

• When Preparation Meets Opportunity

Can anything beat the woman who is prepared up to the eyeballs when a golden opportunity plops in her lap?

Consider: Pia Zadora had been an actress since childhood when she met and married her multi-millionaire husband. He bought movies for her to star in, but she could do it because she was prepared by experience. She: prepared. He: opportunity.

Consider: A college student who sat in on several of my television shows just to get the feel of a station in action was there the night a script assistant didn't show up. Panic everywhere. Don't worry, said Joanne, I can do it. And she did. She had observed and absorbed enough and was ready to go. She: prepared. Late script assistant: opportunity.

As a result of the same meticulous preparedness, Joanne is now a producer. She did her homework, and when the "luck" landed at her feet she could pick it up and run with it. Opportunity, as I never tire of telling everyone, always comes disguised as hard work.

There is no way of knowing what stunning opportunities will come your way; but you won't be able to have a nibble at them if you're not prepared. When they were frantically casting around for an actress to play Scarlett O'Hara in *Gone With The Wind*, Vivien Leigh just happened to be visiting the set. It was a golden opportunity for her: although she was an established stage and screen actress in Britain, she was unknown in America. She'd done her homework, and opportunity handed her stardom.

● *Improper Channels*

I'm sure I have sent out two thousand letters and résumés in my lifetime pursuing jobs and trying to interest producers and agents. I have never got even one job through these normal channels.

In New York I landed an interview with a major network executive. I was so primed for that interview, I was like a loaded gun looking for a target.

"Siddown," the Big Exec growled at me as I swanned into his office on a wave of Chanel and Ban (nerves, you know).

He didn't get up. He didn't even look up. He kept his eyes resolutely glued to the papers on his desk while I rattled on about my past experience and training and talent. No response; his eyes stayed down. I was talking directly to the top of his bald head.

"Oh, and by the way," I tossed off nonchalantly, "I'm a transvestite."

Big Exec sat bolt upright and stared as I kept rattling on about summer stock and my animal series. He didn't say a word. He just scribbled the names of three other people I could see and asked his secretary to get me out of his office—while he watched from a safe distance behind his desk!

Well, I couldn't interest him at all, but one of the three contacts he passed on landed me an agent in New York who got me eight commercial jobs!

Improper channels are dynamite if you've got what I call "skills plus": the necessary skills and the courage to try something different.

When Barbra Streisand was just another unheard-of New York singer, she auditioned for a Broadway role along with hundreds of other unknowns. How could she make the producers, who saw a stream of faces and heard a swarm of voices for ten hours a day, remember her?

When her number was called, she strolled toward the stool on stage, enveloped in a tattered raccoon coat. Mid-stage she shrugged it off and let it drop, all the while noisily chewing a huge wad of gum. Before she started into her number, she slowly and deliberately took the gum out and stuck it under the seat of the stool. The producers were riveted by her audacity. While she sang she had their rapt attention. After she left the casting director couldn't resist checking out that gum. There was none: The whole performance had been a mime to get their attention. It fixed her in the producers' minds forever. Her audacity plus her enormous talent have made her the superstar she is.

Maybe you can't make such a dramatic statement, but you can make a statement.

A friend of mine always wears something slightly offbeat to job interviews to make employers remember her. Sometimes it's a plaid tie, or a man's cap, or a flower in her buttonhole, or pink gloves. People remember a touch of the eccentric, and if you've got talent and skills to match, they're charmed and impressed.

Of course, you can't do this without bags of confidence, but if you've been paying attention you should be overflowing with it by now. Talent gives you the license to be bold. Assurance gives you the flair, the right to be ever-so-slightly outlandish. Leonard once had a woman appear for an interview wearing two different shoes. "Both pairs were so pretty," she said, she couldn't decide which was her favorite. Today she's his top salesperson.

Another woman was interviewed by a national magazine for the job of food writer. She brought her list of credentials, including a Home Economics degree, with her, plus a big chocolate cake. The editors loved them—her and the cake. She got the job.

• Don't Go into the Boxing Ring without Your Gloves On

Now, just a quick word about not going out there naive and fluttery and lost and wandering.

Before you tackle the tough guys, get what you need: skills, equipment, training, experience (if possible), information, and contacts.

It's not easy, I know. You have to take it one baby step at a time, especially if you're starting out after years in the spectators' seats.

A few rules of thumb: If it's the business world you're tackling, you already know what degrees or qualifications you need to do the work you want to do. But nobody will tell you the unwritten rules of that jungle out there. What did I know about the business world? When I was growing up, I learned how to play the piano and make a salmon soufflé. But I've learned a few things since then, and I'll share them with you.

The bottom line in business is always profit. It doesn't matter if one of your co-workers is very difficult to work with. If he delivers for the company, the company loves him, so don't try and fight him. Work around him, and maybe one day you'll work above him.

If you're the only woman working with a group of men, and you're occasionally repelled by their personalities, morals, tactics, and attempts to undermine you, remember: If you can deliver, the company loves you and wants you, and your job is secure.

Unhook your emotions from your job. Don't make the classic "female" error of getting tied in knots of jealousy and pettiness. Women tend to take slights and insults and hostility (all everyday occurrences in business) very seriously. They think someone is "doing the dirty" on them, and they brand that person an enemy for life.

Men realize that today's enemy is tomorrow's ally in business. They take the knives out of their backs with a smile. I'll always remember Leonard ranting and raving about some business deal in which he felt he'd been cut to ribbons. I immediately wanted to take out a contract on the beast that had done such a thing.

"Are you kidding?" Leonard said. "We're partners in a big deal closing next week."

"How can you be," I demanded, "after what he's done to you?" Said Leonard, "The guy's good at what he does. I need him this time around, but I'll get even on the next deal."

A woman would have stabbed her opponent a hundred times with poisoned knitting needles rather than be "partners" with a snake. Not men. They know business is business. Women should learn.

Don't forget to keep your eye on the big picture. Many women, grateful to have come so far and determined to continue to prove their worth, absorb themselves completely in the details of their jobs, while ignoring the broader political picture. Career success depends not just on doing your job well but on how well you play the game. (A must-read: *Games Mother Never Taught You* by Betty Harrigan.) Be aware of the paths to promotion. Pay attention to professional alignments that can work for you and against you. Make sure management knows the full value of what you can do and where you want to go.

Any game is more fun when you understand the rules.

A word about a serious career chase: Excellence in your chosen field requires planning, and that means mapping out the next five (ten?) years of your life.

Do you want to give this much commitment to your job? Are there cities where you will relocate but not others? Are there courses you will have to take in one, two, three years' time to move on? Whose favor should you be currying at the company to make sure you're heading in the direction you want to go? Know what shape you want your career to take before some wise guy at head office tells you.

● The Truth about Success

Success is not a path leading right up to happiness's door. It often brings nerve-twisting, gut-wrenching anxiety.

Judith Krantz told me that when she had signed a contract for $5 million for an as-yet-unwritten book, she was depressed for a month and couldn't write a word.

Success brings its own nightmares. Am I good enough? What if they find out I'm a fraud? (This from a pop singer who got $10,000 a night for a concert.) It drags out every insecurity, every bit of miserable self-doubt lurking under our skins.

"The higher up the ladder I went, the more people's attitudes changed toward me as a woman," recounts one executive friend of mine at the station. "I used to be bright and strong; suddenly I was seen as opinionated and bitchy. The assumption was always that something ugly and masculine took over when women reached the top. I think half the staff thought I had a mustache and smoked a cigar in my office."

Behavior that is applauded in a man may be criticized in a woman. Where a businessman would be called aggressive, a businesswoman is called pushy. He's firm; she's stubborn. He's discriminating; she's prejudiced. He's authoritative; she's hard to work for. He's tough;

she's a bitch. Sometimes it seems that a woman can't win.

The truth about success is that many women still fear it or at least are ambivalent about it. These women believe that true femininity and high achievement are mutually exclusive. A smart woman is caught in a double bind. She fears failure and success equally. If she fails, she hasn't met her own standards of performance. If she succeeds, the price may be loneliness and rejection by men. (Men don't like "tough" women.) Society plays up to this fear. Until recently successful career women were portrayed in books, movies, and television as ruthless, selfish bitches headed for a life without love.

As a result of their ambivalence, women run into other problems.

A friend of mine has worked as an accountant for the same company for twenty years. She is superb at her job, has a big office and a dear secretary, and wields some power in the company. One day, while passing by her boss's office, she overheard this conversation:

"That Sheila is a wonderful accountant; she's turned this company around."

"Yes, she's my best employee. If she were a man I'd be paying her $10,000 a year more. She's worth it."

"If she's worth it, why don't you pay her?"

"Because she's never asked."

Sheila was deliberately undervalued by the company she'd worked for because she didn't know and assert her own worth.

Don't undermine your own worth; there are enough people out there who will try to do it for you. Have you ever noticed that when you come up with what you think is a spectacular new idea and bounce it off the people around you, you hear six different reasons why it can't be done, why you're wasting your time, and why you're foolish to try? I operate on this principle: *The trouble with advice is that it usually interferes with your plans.* Watch out for social sabotage, often coming from the people closest to you. They have an invest-ment in your staying the way you are, in maintaining the status quo. My suggestion is: Discuss your idea with one or two people whom you trust, but in the end follow your gut instinct.

Now, dare we stop concentrating quite so much on you for just a moment and devote some time to the other half of the human race?

I like them, I love them, I've worked and played with them, but it has taken me years to even begin to under-stand them . . . men.

VI

Men: Making the Connection

• Can't Live with Them, Can't Live without Them

Is there any woman out there with breath in her body who hasn't been ready to hang herself with macramé from her plant-lined balcony or throw herself headfirst into the food processor because of a man?

The thought of him not calling, or calling and saying what you don't want to hear, or saying one thing and doing another drives you so crazy you swear you'll never get involved with another one of these swaggering creatures again. But the thought of never having another man to drive you crazy drives you even more crazy.

That old feminist saying that "a woman needs a man like a fish needs a bicycle" is contradicted by everything I see in the women (and men) around me. I cherish the memory of a very good girlfriend of mine swearing, after weeks of crying her heart out over some Casanova, that she'd never, never go near a man again; but she was painting her face and splashing on perfume before a big party, "just in case."

I cannot imagine life without men. They are our fathers, brothers, sons, lovers and husbands (hopefully one and the same!), and the fathers of our children. Despite all the awful ways they clutter up a woman's life—with extra laundry, weekend sports, infidelities, and whiskers in the sink—I wouldn't be without them.

To say we all experience a mixed bag of emotions over the opposite sex is an understatement. How's "fed up," "ripped off," "disillusioned," and "disappointed" versus "ecstatic," "overjoyed," "content," and "fulfilled?" If you start to hate one man, it's easy to hate the lot. If you find one good one, you realize how truly wonderful they can be.

I can flip back through the faces now like flipping through an old photo album. Oh yeah, there was that lizard who promised diamonds and delivered rhinestones; there's that low-life who talked marriage while dating my fourth best friend, and there's that tightwad who thought if he got everything he was after on the first date he wouldn't have to pay for a second. But I don't have to tell you. You've been out with all these guys, right?

Of course, there's also the wonderful man who picked me up in an antique sports car with the entire jumpseat filled with fresh flowers; and that divine Mr. Almost-Right who took me on a mellow autumn afternoon to a nearby resort and paid local actors to dress up like butlers and maids serving tea and reciting love poetry in the garden; and that charming darling who let me ruin his best angora sweater by crying nonstop on it for hours when I was going through terrible trauma. Bless them all!

But when I look back on those single years, I realize I never understood men at all. It's taken me years to figure them out.

When I was a bride of nineteen I truly knew nothing about men, nothing about my own husband.

There was no place to get experience. My father was so busy supporting the family that we had little time together. My brother was years younger than I was, and I had already gone away to university before he was an adolescent. My husband was my first serious boyfriend and lover. I started to learn about men when I stepped into the singles life at the age of thirty-three, and for a long time I thought it was one class in life where I'd always be wearing the dunce cap.

After several disastrous forays into the dating scene, I resigned myself to being single forever and concentrated all my energy on my kids and career. But the oddest thing happened. As soon as I took over my own life, as soon as I started to feel my own strength and said a final "hasta la vega" to the Prince Charming myth, the right kind of men started turning up in my life.

It taught me my first lesson in understanding men: They don't want a clingy woman, a neurotic woman, a depressed or desperate woman. Confidence is a kind of aphrodisiac. I don't know why I found this so surprising: I certainly never wanted a clingy, neurotic, depressed, or desperate man.

I also discovered, much to my shock (don't forget, I grew up when the most desirable men were sort of Conan the Barbarian with Cadillacs), that many of the ruthless, cool men I met in public had a gentle, almost feminine side to them in private. I liked that.

The men I was drawn to turned to the women in their lives to draw out that sensitive side, to let their emotions out after a day of hard-headed reasoning. I found it appealing and lovable and endearing and sexy.

Perhaps the greatest lesson I learned was that a man doesn't complete you. You complete yourself.

After one marriage, a couple of relationships, and dates who could be described as wild, boring, incredible, ridiculous, mean, amusing, cheap, dipsy, kind, erratic, and affectionate, I concluded that it is better to live with a man than without one. But he had to be the right one.

He had to be not *a* man, but *the* man.

When you find a dear man who loves all the ways you are different from him, not just the same, who values your work as much as his own, who sees you as an independent person, not just an extension of himself, who will share your soul (if you let him) but will never claim ownership—well, all I can say is: Soak it up like a sponge, because it's as good as life gets.

• What Do You Want in a Man?

Would you believe that on the brink of singledom, when a friend asked me that, I couldn't answer?

When I sat down to make a list, I had nothing to write.

Life used to be simple: In high school the number-one quality we all looked for in a man was that he look like Troy Donahue! In my twenties who thought about men? I was married. I had a husband. When I found myself in the position of looking for another, I didn't know what I wanted to find.

Trial and error (trial by ordeal would be more accurate) enlightened me on a few I didn't want.

For instance, I definitely showed the door to the bank manager who brought an overnight bag to Sunday brunch on the assumption he'd be staying until Monday morning. Ditto to the car rally enthusiast whose idea of heaven was sitting at the edge of a dusty track for hours while noisy vehicles went brum-brum-brum around the circuit. The same goes for the film buff whose idea of a night at the movies was *The Texas Chainsaw Massacre* followed by *The Thing* followed by *Bruce Lee and the King of Kung-Fu.* I mean, our tastes were just too different even though he did look like Paul Newman in the dim light of the theater.

Each man brings his own surprise package.

Pauline, a young sales clerk in my favorite dress store, told me that she was sure she'd found Mr. Right until the first night he slept over—and he got up at five a.m. to do primal yodeling. "It was like being awakened by Tarzan in agony with a kidney stone," she said. "He claimed it was basic primal therapy and he needed it to get his spirit on line for the day. I asked him to pack his loincloth and swing off the balcony forever."

The guy you show to the door (or balcony) may be another woman's dream.

When I told the story of Pauline's Tarzan to a woman in my exercise class, her eyes lit up with absolute lust. She imagined herself his Jane.

Some women adore flatterers (even when they know it's not all true, it makes them feel good); others fall for tough-talking, independent, hard-to-hold types. I've seen intelligent, assertive women cry like babies over some womanizer who wouldn't spare them a kind word and soft, clingy, female creatures captivate hard-nosed, ruthless business tycoons. They've obviously found some touchstone in each other and are joyously on their way to happily ever after . . . or at least to the middle of next week. (As Roberta Flack says, "I used to believe forever lasted at least two years.")

There's often a yawning gap between what women want in a first relationship and what they demand the second time around.

Marcia explains: "In my first marriage all I cared about was that I loved the guy. He was handsome and loving, and I didn't care about anything else, including the fact that he was out of work and we lived in a crummy bachelor apartment up three flights of stairs with no elevator. Who cared about such trivia? I was in love. As long as we slept in the same bed at night I was happy. Now he's split, and I've smartened up. I want some of the luxury I missed. The next man has to be self-supporting with a good salary: I want to see the inside of a few restaurants and theaters and cruise ships. I won't live like a poor little church mouse again."

Deborah couldn't disagree more. "I've had all that," she said. "We had a gorgeous house, trips to Europe, accounts at every classy store in town. And he was a bastard. All I care about, if I ever hook up with another man, is that he's gentle and honest and loving and considerate. I don't want things, I want him."

Well, ladies, it looks like you have a choice of paths. Personally, I'd take the middle one: one that likes to be comfortable in life—a glass of champagne on a Southern beach isn't so injurious to true love. But you want to share it with someone who will kiss you after the cork pops and who knows how to rub jojoba oil into your skin in his own special way.

Although I'm sure there are a lot of men and women who still believe that picking a mate is simply luck, I say it's easier to get what you want if you have some idea of what you're looking for. At least you'll recognize it when you see it, and you can express how much you admire and value those qualities in another human being. Praise does wonderful things for a man's sense of hearing.

I often think of Gloria Swanson's response to the question of why she married six times. She said, "All I wanted as a child was to be grown up, wear a wedding ring, be married, and have twelve children. Somehow I couldn't quite picture the man at the other end of the dinner table." It was never clear in her own mind what she was looking for in a man and what, in fact, she really needed as a woman.

It's easy to be bedazzled by the gorgeous guy who does a mad tango, spends oodles of money, and drives a sexy car. But after the honeymoon is over and all the facades drop away, there'd better be the inner stuff that makes for compatible day-to-day living. On my "must have" list are trustworthiness, sense of humor, intelligence, and shared values. What's on yours?

My girlfriend Christine says her list hasn't helped her at all in her never-ending quest for Mr. Right. "What's on it?" I asked. "He has to be powerful, handsome, sensitive, intelligent, charming, rich, dependable, extroverted, sensual, witty, idealistic, virile, moralistic, socially conscious, articulate, a vegetarian, and have a great bum in jeans!" Need I say more!!!

Why do women still persist in thinking that they need a man to take care of them? The answer is simple:

Because it's easier—because it's part of the fairy tale with the happy ending, and we all want happy endings. Not only that, it saves you from doing too much heavy-duty thinking or facing the reality when the bills and toilet have all backed up. Believing a man will always take care of you serves to keep you cushioned, co-cooned, and protected. Perhaps some women are lucky enough to slip through most of a lifetime with someone else in the driver's seat; the message that they have to look after themselves never hits them on the head until life hits them on the head.

I'm no exception to the rule. When I was separated, financially and emotionally at my wit's end, and over-burdened with responsibility, I still clung to the "happily ever after" myth. Wistfully I would conjure up a clouded image of someone, somehow, saving me from rough waters, pulling my poor little dinghy over and attaching it to a big ship, and everything would be okay.

If the truth be known, the person who finally answered my SOS was me. What I had to do was learn to make my own happy ending. As long as I held on to the fantasy that somehow a man would take care of me, the transaction of meeting and going out with someone I liked was doomed from the start. It's amazing how, even with someone you hardly know, you fantasize that this man has the wonderful strength to lift you up and out. By investing your fantasies in him, you automatically give him power over you and set up an imbalance from day one—not to mention the very heavy expectations you lay on this poor male soul.

Here are some dead giveaways that you are still frantically shopping around for a "White Knight take care of me for life" endowment policy. Before the end of the third date:

• You buy him a wildly inappropriate gift—a ring, a watch, a weekend for two (guess which two) at the Seahorse Snuggle Inn, home of the vibrating water bed.

- You insist he read beddy-bye stories to your kids.
- You express too much interest in the extra closet space in his apartment.
- You insist he come to a cousin's weekend and meet the entire family.
- You automatically gravitate toward the kitchen and laundry room (his or yours) and start darning socks and baking cookies.
- You make in-depth inquiries about his financial status.
- You ask if he has any allergies to pets or kids.
- You spend seven out of eight hours fantasizing about this near-stranger: You're either on an erotic weekend or attending a PTA meeting together.
- You dreamily mention your thoughts to your kids, and they repeat their version of it to him. "Mom says you might be our new Dad."

If you give off any or all of these vibes, the invisible sign plastered across your forehead, "Feed me, I'm yours!" becomes visible, and your Mr. Wonderful will run as fast as possible in the opposite direction.

As an adult woman you can "take care of" yourself. When you really believe that, your behavior changes and you give off a different set of signals that men pick up and respond to in a positive way. You now have a reasonable expectation that he may choose to fulfill, which is to "care for" you. And if he does, and you choose to respond, your relationship will be based on a much healthier mutuality from the start.

• What Do Men Want?

One of my first dates when I started playing "singles" was, appropriately enough, fixed up by a fellow member of our tennis club.

"Micki, you'll love this guy," Jack assured me. "He's a tennis nut, and he's always looking for a new partner."

Great, I thought, a healthy afternoon of sunny skies

and clean competition. This man was a tennis nut, all right—knew every score of every match played at Wimbledon since 1900!—but he was a terrible player. I didn't care, but he sure did.

"You didn't have a good time, did you?" I asked as he drove me home after three sets.

"I didn't know you played so well," he said stiffly.

"I thought after talking to Jack that you wanted someone to play tennis with," I said.

"I did—but I didn't want someone who could win."

Is there any answer to that?

At least, I thought as I watched him drive off, there goes a man who knows what he wants—a loser.

Ask most men what they want, and they're as vague as most women: They're after someone who is "terrific," "warm," "beautiful," "sexy"—but what does that mean?

Dr. Joyce Brothers, the guru of women's magazines, insists that all men are attracted first, foremost, and always to physical beauty and that everything else comes second, fifth, and twenty-third. Many men say sexiness is what first attracts them and often keeps them. Very few men have I ever heard say that brains, compassion, humor, vitality is what first drew them to a woman; she had to be physically exciting first, and then they noticed she was funny, intelligent, and capable.

I have asked literally hundreds of men about what they want in a woman, and although they struggle to put their ideal female into words—it is hard to conjure up a woman with Jane Fonda's legs, Dolly Parton's breasts, Julia Child's kitchen skills, Xaviera Hollander's bedroom skills, and Indiana Jones's stamina—they are very definite about what turns them off.

Are they talking about you here?

- "I resent being put in the 'all men are chauvinists' category."
- "I abhor clinging women who sit like baby birds in

143

the nest with their mouths open waiting for a man to feed them."

• "I hate being number two, just behind her job schedule."

• "I hate women who willingly go to bed, then reproach themselves the next morning with: 'Oh God, how could I have done that, you must think I'm a tramp,' etc., etc."

• "I'm sick of women who spend the entire evening—which I'm paying for—moaning about past love affairs or their divorce and laying all the sentimental baggage on the table before we even know if there's going to be a second date."

• "I run from women who start talking immediately about their biological time clock running out."

• "I don't call women again if they're deliberately passive in bed—you know, lying there with a sort of 'Well, come on, fella, do your stuff' challenge. It's a real turn-off."

• "I have trouble with women who are attracted to me because I am a tough, successful businessman and then expect me to switch gears at the end of the day and become soft, nurturing, and sensitive. It's a large order to fill."

• "I hate women whose first question is: 'So what's your sign?' "

• "I despise women who judge a man by the size of his wallet." One rather serious-looking bachelor I know sums it up this way: "When I'm at a party and I mention I had a hard day at the hospital, a bevy of beauties gathers round. (There's a single doctor on the loose!) When I clarify that I work on the hospital kitchen staff, they scatter faster than a gaggle of geese."

Of course, none of these apply to you, but you might have a friend, right?

The more I talk to men and women, the more I am faced with the reality that sexiness and beauty are the hooks that reel them in.

This was making me suicidal until an astute and lovely man put it in perspective for me.

"You're just thinking of breasts and bottoms when you think of sex appeal," he said accusingly. (Well, what does *he* think of—chopped liver?) "Actually, sexiness goes beyond that for men: It's whatever it is about the woman that inspires his feelings of sexiness and fantasy. It could be the perfume of a plain woman or the lacy edge of a camisole peeking out from under her blouse. Something about her generates physical excitement.

"I have fallen in love with a woman because of her laugh. It was the one distinctive characteristic I remembered and carried around with me all day. It's an association game. She laughed this beautiful laugh in bed, and when I thought of her—even though she wasn't particularly attractive—I thought of the laugh and the circumstances, and I just had to see her again."

Since this adorable man said this, I have been practicing laughing until Leonard thinks he is living with a hyena.

Seriously, I think there are some basic things men want and need. As you consider these, remember: It's one thing to talk about what all men want, but the important thing is: What does *your* man want? The best way to find out is to talk to him and listen to him.

• Respect him. His ego is like eggshell. Don't belittle or criticize him in public or any way but delicately in private; men hate being made to feel foolish or awkward the way a cat hates cold water.
• Never make fun (even in fun) of his sexual performance.
• Learn to do one thing he loves (fishing, skiing, sailing) really well. It's such a compliment.
• Give him privacy. If Wednesday night is his night with the boys, make it your night with the girls, or take a class or learn an instrument. Some interests are kept interesting by not sharing them.

- Respect his commitment to his work. As the saying goes: Women love men and men love work. Don't ever tell a man, "It's only a job." That's like saying, "It's only your life."
- Don't insist that a man who loathes the kitchen learn to cook because it's "his turn." It's cheaper to send out for pizza or Chinese food than replace the food processor, the two back burners on the stove, and your best copper pot. Believe me.
- Resign yourself to the fact that there will be a ball of some size and shape that he will either chase around himself or spend hours watching others do it.
- Accept the fact that there will always be some flaw in your wonderful man that will drive you to the edge of Splitsville. It might be leaving a ring around the tub, taking three weeks to change a burned-out light bulb, or last-minute surprises of the "Didn't I tell you it's the office party tonight?" type. If no amount of negotiating changes this flaw, treat it as a lovable idiosyncrasy. It's not worth paying two lawyers green fees for a year to get a divorce and then find a new man with some other shtick to drive you crazy.
- It's unfair to expect a man, even the wonderful, exciting love of your life, to supply your every emotional need—to fill you with excitement, fulfillment, happiness, and joy. You are fifty percent of your relationship, so put in your share.
- It is very unfair and unrealistic to expect a man to be as crazy as a woman and give up every other friend in the world so he can spend every precious second of every day with you. Many woman do this. I have "friends" I see only between men.

Men don't do this. They want those Saturday mornings on the baseball diamond with the company team. (Yes, they want it as much as they want to snuggle under satin sheets and nibble croissants and strawberries with you.) Don't make your relationship a series of choices of which you are always one. Give the guy a chance to find out how much he misses you.

A man wants a woman who makes him feel good about himself—not just about the exterior things (that hair transplant looks wonderful, Harry) but also about the vital, soul-sustaining, interior things, too. I think he wants his woman to understand the hidden part of him, the tender, vulnerable part he can't expose to his buddies or at the board meeting. Recognizing this hidden part can be a wise woman's greatest strength. He might call it his weakness; a woman who loves him would call it his humanity, and her love enables him to express it.

This is often like panning for gold. It's back-breaking work. But dig away. It's worth it, because then a man can feel he is being loved and cherished and wanted not just for what he can buy, but for who he is. He probably hasn't spent much time in his life worrying about who he is. A woman who can open him up to a new kind of sensitivity is his for life. He needs her.

• Men Are Equal but Different

Eons ago, when I was a naive, foolish little soul, I used to think men and women operated on the same level, with the same principles and the same understanding of the world.

Expecting a man to react to life the way a woman does is like expecting the family dog to prepare Eggs Benedict on Sunday morning and serve the family in bed.

It might happen on the moon, but not here.

Baby men start life being different from baby women. Girl babies are naturally more responsive to people: They smile more often, they respond to other infants crying, and they show more interest in a real human face than boy babies do.

Sociological studies reveal that mothers cuddle, pet, and hug boy babies less than girl babies (don't want to create a little sissy, do we?). As they grow up boys are encouraged to be rough, tough, aggressive, on the winning team. Girls are taught to get along with others, share, and pay attention to their feelings and the feelings of others.

Girls can steal from boys: It's neat to be an eight-year-old tomboy fishing for tadpoles, but it definitely isn't neat, if you're a boy, to dress up little dolls and play house. A boy lives with the demand to grow up "to be a man" hanging over him from the cradle.

The point of this treatise is that we, men and women, are so different in our approach to life, it's a wonder we ever get together at all.

Things are changing slowly: Men are realizing it's okay to open up and be sensitive, and women are getting tougher and more success-oriented.

Men are not only emotionally different from us; they are also sexually different. Now here's a trouble-starter: Men say honestly they can have a one-night stand with a woman, enjoy it, and forget it. It means nothing. It is purely physical, there is no emotional entanglement, not even for a second. Women tend to want to feel something tender, even if it isn't cataclysmic love.

Men are on such a different wavelength. Women who don't understand this can spend the rest of their lives trying to change something that can't be changed.

A friend once said to me, "Micki, I just want a man to listen to me." That's a big request, because men haven't been raised to listen. Geared to success, they are used to being assertive, making points, and being listened to. Women, on the other hand, are trained from birth to ask questions and hang on a man's every word.

Women want men to be wildly, crazily romantic and book off Monday morning to spend another illicit day in bed. Men can't fathom this, no matter how much in love they are: Business is business.

Women have memories. I can remember in photographic detail the music, the clothes, the whispered conversations of those special, romantic evenings. I read about a couple who on their anniversary recreated the moment they met, wearing the same clothes, returning to the street where they crossed paths with each other. They had tea in the same restaurant and replayed the same conversation, rekindling the electricity of those first moments. What a wonderful idea, I thought. So one night I prepared my husband's favorite meal, put on Sonny James's "Young Love" in the background, and wore my wedding dress to the table. He looked up at me with loving eyes and said, "Have I seen that dress before?"

Keep telling yourself that for all their peculiarities men aren't more or less than women, just different. Humor them sometimes, fight with them, love them, and try and understand them. It's a lifetime project, but, believe me, the research is a lot of fun!

• Where to Meet Men

There are thousands of them out there, so why isn't there just one in your life? Well, it's been said a million times, but saying it once more can't hurt: You won't meet any men sitting alone in your room reading Gothic romances or practicing yoga or baking shortbread. Get out there!

I can't, you say. I can't just wander the streets like a dogcatcher looking for stray animals. Of course not. But don't you have dozens of reasons to be out there anyway? My spies handed over lists of their own "best places" to meet men (all tried, true, and tested):

- Jogging.
- Walking a dog (number one on a dozen lists).
- Art galleries and museums.
- Browsing in bookstores.
- Spectator sports.
- Supermarkets on Saturday afternoons.
- Sailing classes (very good; flying and skiing classes are also good).
- Night school, especially the "masculine" classes like woodworking and home handyman. (What's wrong

with learning to fix a broken toaster while you're fixing a broken heart?)

- Political events.
- Investment seminars.
- Computer courses.
- Martial arts classes.
- Lineups at the movies, the liquor store, or the bank.
- Hospitals, doing volunteer work.
- The great outdoors (hiking, scuba classes, environmental courses or causes).

I'll add a few from my own experience. One time when my leg was in a cast, I couldn't hobble half a block without some muscle-bound male rushing up to see if he could assist in any way. (Another time I ended up with a black eye, but that's another story.) I have a T-shirt that says, "Robert Redford begged me to make love to him, but I wouldn't." Talk about a conversation starter.

A girlfriend of mine, determined to make contact with a stunning specimen who was browsing the rare wine racks, "accidentally" dented his fender (ever so slightly) in the parking lot. What choice did he have? Names and telephone numbers were exchanged, and he was invited over for a "forgive me" drink. He came, she conquered, they had a blissful romance for a few hot summer months, and she didn't have to pay for the fender!

I still giggle when I recall walking down the street with Lance and passing a gorgeous man whom I'd seen around the neighborhood and been too shy to approach. Dropping over to borrow a cup of Minute Rice didn't seem right. I worried for nothing. Gorgeous Man stopped me (and Lance) on the street and asked, "Hey, haven't I seen you on television?" I preened and glowed. "Aren't you the woman in the milk of magnesia commercial?"

"Yeah," piped up darling little Lance, "she's the constipated one."

I have found men (or they have found me) in the unlikeliest places.

I was driving down the highway once when a car pulled alongside; the driver was gesturing wildly at my front tire. I pulled over onto the shoulder, leaped out, and so did a bald Japanese man.

"What is it?" I demanded frantically. "What's wrong with my car?"

"Nothing, madam," he replied, "but I think you are very attractive, and I'd like to take you out for a coffee."

"But I'm married," I said. (I was at the time.)

"So am I."

"Nothing doing." I jumped back in my car and roared off, wondering why it's always miniature married men in these encounters and never Robert Goulet.

A few days later I was dropping off a résumé at one of the TV networks when a man grabbed me from behind, lifted me off my feet, spun me around, and kissed me full on the lips!

"Oh, God, sorry," he said when he came up for air, "I thought you were someone else."

I was staring into the heavenly blue eyes of—you guessed it—Robert Goulet!

"But," he continued before I could change myself into whomever he wanted me to be, "can I buy you a drink anyway?"

Of course I did what any respectable married woman would do—I said "Sure." He was a charmer. We had a drink, and he gave my husband and me two front-row tickets to *Camelot*.

Of course, when women talk about meeting men what they mean is meeting the right man.

A perfectly good airplane trip was ruined for me by a heavy lecher in the next seat. For five hours he leaned on me, breathed on me, made sexy suggestions, told me how wonderful he was, how women couldn't resist him. I mean, this guy was like a ton of slimy bricks. When the plane touched down he slipped out his little black book and rasped in my ear: "Here is my secret

151

book of the world's loveliest women. Put your name and phone number in here, and I'll probably call."

A look of quiet, cocky satisfaction spread over his face as I scribbled in the book.

I would like to have seen his reaction when he opened the page later and read: "I will meet you at three a.m. in the bus station in Thunder Bay. You'll really enjoy me. I have three breasts."

But the Cock-of-the-Walk award goes to the guy who actually said, "Women are like flies, and I'm the Vapona strip!" A few of these incidents might be enough to send you back to your Gothic romances. But I used to treat them as potential comedy sketches, and I didn't close up shop on the singles scene. Attitude is everything!

More great places to meet men: through friends; at singles clubs, groups, and bars. I know you're going to shriek: "Not singles bars!" But they don't have to be those meat market scenes. Many chic restaurants have a cosy bar at the front where you and a girlfriend can have a glass of wine and survey the fair gentlemen with their elbows on the bar (and perhaps their eyes on you). Singles groups that organize dances, outings, and nights on the town are not to be sneered at. At least you all know something about each other: You're single, available, and interested. It doesn't hurt to try.

Personal ads and dating services are becoming more popular. One woman explained to me that getting four or five answers to her ad makes her feel in control. She's the one who decides whom to call.

Her experience has been that the men who reply to these ads are genuine, but she offers some ground rules for novices: Always include a box number, not your address or telephone numbeer; meet your potential date in a very public place; exercise every bit of personal judgment, common sense, and intuition you've got to weed out the weirdos. If you don't want to do this alone, place an ad for brunch with a group of your single friends.

Of course, meeting men and dating when you have children is a whole different kettle of gefilte fish. My children, through their own natural adorableness, have scuttled my social life many times. I vividly recall telling Lance that the man who was coming over one evening was a real success story.

He'd had a terrible childhood, had been in trouble with the law, and had even gone to jail for stealing a car. But he'd educated himself, put himself through university, and was now a highly placed executive with a television network. When the man arrived, Lance greeted him at the door with, "So you're the car thief."

Lisa did her share, too. With the dining room table set for dinner for two and the best silver glowing in the candlelight, Lisa looked wistfully from the table to my guest and murmured, "Gee, at least *you* get a decent meal around here."

The most important thing, however you decide to track a man down, is that you do it cheerfully, in good humor, and with high spirits.

There's a lot of talk about the great man shortage, and it does seem sometimes that every man you know is married, divorced with heavy problems, in love with someone else, or gay. The only solution is to find one more man: your man.

The thing to remember is that men are out there waiting to be met. Some of them are slightly less threatening than Dracula, some are just looking for someone to sleep with, some are looking for someone to talk to— but remember that they are looking. And so are you. So keep believing you'll get together.

Out there, right now, doing his shopping at the market (four pounds of kolbassa, three pounds of potato salad) or picking up his shirts from the laundry (folded and starched) or wandering through the medieval section at the art gallery is your man, just waiting for you.

So shave your legs, get fresh coffee in the house, and go find him. Then get ready for some real problems. If life is complicated without a man, it's labyrinthine with one.

• Why Do I Still Think He Has to Be Older than, Smarter than, Richer than, Taller than Me?

When I first started dating I had this bee in my brain that the Great Elusive had to be older than, smarter than, richer than, taller than me—I mean, doesn't that just define a man? It's a dusty, creaking definition, and after a very short ride on the dating merry-go-round I threw it away forever.

I did crash through the social taboo barrier by dating a younger man. This charming young man was seven years my junior and a law student (at least he wasn't an art student or something really outré).

He was pleasant company, but how long could it last between two people when one is worried about his exams and the other is worried about her kids' braces?

He also didn't have an enormous amount of money, which made it awkward; he used to put our dates on his father's credit cards, and in the end I decided his father couldn't afford me.

"Micki, how can you? Think of the children," a friend admonished.

"I did think of them. Maybe they and my new young friend could play together after school."

Not being the only "cradle snatcher" in my circle, I polled some other "older women" and compared notes. Younger men appeared to be less threatened by our success or personality and less afraid to show their feelings than a man a generation older.

They're more willing to share, more easygoing, and less intimidated by an assertive woman. They tend to be more nurturing. They can be dynamite in bed, with more energy and vigor.

If that's the case, why aren't thousands of older women swooping down like ravens on available younger men?

There are drawbacks.

If he's very young you have to explain who Gene Kelly and Fred Astaire are when the late show is on.

They think garter belts are sexy, while every woman old enough to remember the pre-pantyhose days thinks of them as a nuisance and loathes them.

And as a prominent writer once commented, "Dating a younger man means constantly holding in your stomach."

Dorothy was hung up on a different taboo. She swore she wouldn't date anyone shorter than her five feet ten inches. She felt ridiculous. The last time I saw her in New York, she was raving about her new man. I couldn't understand it: He barely came up to her shoulder.

"What happened?" I asked her. "He opened his mouth," she beamed. "He's so bright and charming and well-educated and a delight to listen to. When he talks he's six feet tall to me."

Many women still believe that a man has to be smarter. (How else is he going to be richer?) Women have been trained to marry up, not down, the scale. Through marriage a woman attains her status, security, and identity. For years men have chosen women for a variety of reasons: their warmth, their sensitivity, their sensuality, their wit. You have the same privilege.

Whoa! Micki, what man? you ask. I can't find any man—shorter, balder, poorer, fatter, dumber. I am at the point of settling for the man from Glad on his day off.

Cheer up! I know that Saturday night depression. I have eaten my share of chocolate chip cookies alone, weeping and munching through the last movie on the dial.

I started out, as some of you started out, with a lot of lofty notions about dating and misconceptions about men and women.

May I share a few lacerating lessons?

It's a big mistake (but an easy and common one) to view every man you meet as "marriageable material."

Some men aren't for marriage. It doesn't mean they can't be great friends or even lovers.

My friend Donna, who entered the single life about the same time I did, dated conga lines of men in the first year. Most she rejected after the first date.

One date isn't the time to pass judgment forever.

First dates are slightly nervous and hesitant. After all, here are two strangers. Give him a second or third chance, because people don't blossom and reveal their true selves until they're really comfortable and at ease.

Men and women need to feel secure before they drop their facade and just be themselves. If you like him, enjoy his company and just let it be. Let the relationship unfold in its own time. Don't assume all men will work to your timetable.

Don't expect men to be perfect and ideal. That's for the gods on Mount Olympus. We scurrying mortals here on earth can't afford such nobility. This doesn't mean you don't have to have high standards and principles— just make sure that human beings can reach them.

Decide early on why you are dating and what you want from men. This isn't as obvious as it sounds. Some women want a man to "round them off," to complete them, to provide a date for New Year's Eve because everybody else is going out. Some pursue men with one object: matrimony. Others have no interest in a long-term commitment but are after a good time, lots of laughs, and lots of partners.

Which brings me a touchy subject. Women complain that men use them. But a lot of women use men and are harder on them than on their favorite walking pumps.

You use a man when you call him because you have to have a date for the company party, but you don't really like him; when you arrive at a party with him and leave with someone else; when you sleep with him because you haven't had sex for months and you want physical contact; when you know that he is eating his heart out over you and you keep him around because there's no one more interesting.

One other point about dating men: Desperate, anxious, craving women rarely attract anybody they'd really like to be with. Be honest and admit why you really need a date or want a man.

Do you want unconditional love without demands? Get a dog.

Do you want someone who cares and worries about your every move? Visit Mother.

Do you want someone just to squire you around the latest hot spots? Dragoon your kid brother or his friend.

Do you long to pour out your heart and soul nonstop to a sympathetic ear? Pay a shrink or see a minister.

This might be the place to sneak in a word or two about sex. (There's a whole chapter on it coming up.) Single women sometimes enjoy what used to be known as "one-night stands." "Casual sex" sounds so unromantic. The best description I've ever read of these brief, hot encounters is "love snacks." There's no future but a lot of fun in the stopovers on the highway to True Love. Women on their own sometimes need the warmth of physical contact, and if that is what you need, who am I to deny you? But you must be able to get up and sing in the shower the next morning and feel relaxed and comfortable and divine.

If even thinking about it makes you feel grubby or scruffy, it's not for you. Don't try to force it, no matter what your best friend, now devouring her thirty-eighth airline pilot on an overnight stopover, says.

• It's Not What They Say, It's What They Do

My friend Heather was so in love with Terry it was painful to watch. He told her, repeatedly, the one thing she longed to hear from every man she met: "I'll be there for you. When you need me, call."

Well, Heather needed him. She needed him when she lost her job—but he had planned a night out with the boys. She needed him when her old pussycat, companion of twelve years, died, and she was midnight blue. But he was going fishing that weekend. She needed to see him over lunch one day, because their out-of-town business schedules had crisscrossed and they hadn't seen each other for two weeks. But he was lunching with an old buddy, and he didn't want to cancel unless it was really necessary. Terry talked a good show. But his performance was the pits.

What more can one say other than it's true: Talk is cheap. Any man (or woman) can say, "I love you, I'll be there for you, I'll support you, I'm your friend." But if their actions continually make lies of their words, it's time to say bye-bye.

The hints drop early enough. I (almost) fell madly in love with a stockbroker I met at a neighborhood brunch. He seemed honest, sincere, sympathetic, and totally divine (to say nothing of being handsome, rich, and available).

He said he'd call me the next day and we'd get together. I came home from work early and canceled a tennis game to sit, clinging like a barnacle, to the phone.

It didn't ring.

Finally he called a week later and said we'd meet for dinner. He'd pick me up at seven. He arrived at eight.

He was delighted when he found out we had birthdays on the same day. We must do something special. He'd arrange something and call. He never did. Was I sorry? No, I can get older by myself, and I spent the night in front of the television with one candle on my chocolate chip cookie.

That was one of the first things I loved about Leonard. He didn't talk much about plans—he just did things.

Romance without reliability is a liability. Hmm, wonder if I could get that on a bumper sticker?

• A Chase Is Nice: Let It Happen

I am not thinking about a free-for-all around the glass

coffee table (unless that is what you want), but the process of courtship.

If on the first date you declare yourself madly in love, jump into bed, give him your detailed biography, and propose marriage, what are you going to do on the second?

It's lovely to be chased. The simmering excitement that lets you yearn a little makes it all the sweeter when you get "caught."

Really, that word "chase" sounds so old-fashioned. How about something more hard-nosed and modern, like "negotiate?"

There comes a point in any relationship when it becomes serious, when it's not just laughs and kisses, when it occurs to you that this is really going somewhere and the possibility of greater commitment exists.

Now, silent and unspoken, we're into a negotiating process. What have you got to negotiate with? You. You are your number-one chip, so don't undervalue yourself. If this romance is getting serious, set some ground rules and make sure you get what you want and need from the relationship.

Negotiating or chasing—let's call it chasing, it sounds more exciting—can't happen unless you leave room for it. It springs out of a process of discovery about the other person. It takes time and heartfelt interest to find out the other person's secrets and to yield up a few of your own.

He calls you for a date and you're busy. Doing what? he asks. It's Tuesday, you say. It's my photography class.

He didn't know you were interested in photography, but now he does. He can fret for a night while you putter in the darkroom; you'll only be more desirable for the wait.

Sometimes the chase is the old-fashioned, in-hot-pursuit type that used to burn up Humphrey Bogart movies.

I heard a great story about a woman who spotted a stunning man dining alone in a restaurant. She stared so brashly at him that he finally approached her and asked, "Is anything wrong?"

"No," she replied coolly. "It's just that you look so much like my second husband."

"How many times have you been married?"

"Just once."

Women can chase men just like men can chase women. Obviously they can and they will. All chasing in one direction is the quickest way to no deal.

There is something tantalizing and madly thrilling about the early days of courtship when you dance around each other eaten up with desire but coolly holding back to spin out the agony.

It's nice to feel slightly less available than a McDonald's hamburger. It's nice to feel like a much-sought-after, cherished commodity. It's nice for both of you, so give him a few quick races around the block.

Really, when the two of you are in love, it's a mutual chasing. What you do when you catch each other is your business.

• If a Good Man Is Hard to Find, Why Do I Want to Leave the One I've Got?

When Joni Mitchell sang, "You don't know what you've got till it's gone," she wasn't kidding.

So before you abandon old Harry, his fourteen bowling balls, and three pounds of unwashed socks, have a good, long think. You loved this man once, balls, socks, and all, so what happened? When did you start seeing all the things he isn't instead of the adorable things that first bound you together like glue?

A number of women I've talked to want to walk away from their relationships because they're bored.

"There's nothing wrong with Jack. He's a good provider, he's kind, he doesn't drink or run around, but I'm dying."

Believe me, out there a great many single women are dying of boredom, too.

There's nothing riveting about sitting home alone Friday night doing your nails and dreaming of Tom Selleck. And nothing enchanting about dating a string of Don Juans (or Don Harrys). "Men want me either to sleep with them or to do their laundry," one single woman complained, and there's a lot of truth in that lament.

Some relationships do sour and fail, okay. But before you conclude that yours is one of them, perhaps you should try and define the "nothing" in "nothing wrong."

Maybe Harry seems so awful because for the last year you've been concentrating on his faults and forgetting all the times he picked up your mother's groceries, took the kids off your hands so you could go out, offered to take in a movie (when it wasn't bowling night), and suggested he scrub your back in the shower. Can't you remember even three things that once made him Errol Flynn in your eyes?

If you can appreciate what Harry's got, maybe he's still the one for you.

Many women assume that a better man (read richer, smarter, more handsome, older) would give them more and fill their lives with milk and honey. Uh-uh. We've been through this before (gosh, you're stubborn). Men do not put the finishing touches on incomplete little you. Either you do it, or it doesn't get done!

Of course, your sex life would be a million times more thrilling if you were rolling around in the hay (or on Astroturf, for that matter) with—well, fill in your own dream lover: Robert Redford, Jack Nicholson, David Bowie, Boy George . . .

But the likelihood of finding him in your neighborhood convenience store is slim, so don't throw a good, if familiar, relationship over for a fantasy.

I keep telling Leonard I said yes to him only because Redford was busy, and, besides, who wants to live in L.A. anyway? Too much smog.

Also, don't forget this horrible slap of realism: While

you're plotting a gay and glorious life away from your stodgy, boring mate, he may be plotting the same thing. Are you the same sprightly, cheerful, loving woman he fell in love with? Are you caring and considerate, interested in his work, his problems, his happiness? Do you still talk to him about his troubles, do you initiate lovemaking the way you used to, praise him, and show your admiration? You two may have more in common than you want to admit. Why not try and add some spice to your bland diet before you see the lawyer?

A friend of mine saved her marriage (and lawyers' fees) by jazzing up her sex life with her husband. Instead of always Saturday-night-with-the-lights-out-and-when-the-kids-are-asleep, they now get a sitter and go to a motel or ship the kids off to grandma and start the afternoon with a bubble bath.

"It works, because we see each other as exciting lovers again," my friend says, "not just two people sharing a mortgage."

If it works I say: Hurrah!

Nothing as simple and pleasurable as this works when the relationship really is over. Then you've got to face the desperate, difficult ugliness (sorry—for most couples there's no other word) of letting go.

• Why Are You Missing Him Far More Than You Ever Loved Him?

Separations, divorces, partings of any sort are a kind of death. That's not overstating it. It is the death of a relationship, of love and dreams and trust and pleasure.

It isn't nice, it isn't easy, it hurts—so don't expect to feel good about it. Passion is a powerful drug; love is a viciously powerful lifeline, so don't expect to let it go without a fight-to-the-finish struggle in your heart.

When I separated from my husband I felt, even though we both knew we were doing the right thing, that every dream I'd ever held precious had been trampled.

When my friend Bonnie separated from her longtime lover she got in the car and drove nonstop, sobbing and crying and beating the steering wheel. She jokes now she was halfway across the country before she ran out of gas and hankies.

A beautiful actress in town who finally had to let go of her semialcoholic lover said she spent weeks sleeping with four pillows bunched into his body shape beside her so she wouldn't feel so alone. They were all, she swears, sodden with tears.

Nothing can ease that first deep, dark pain of a split except time.

You can help the healing process along, but don't expect, even if you cared only a sliver for him, to escape its agonies completely. Not only are you giving up the person; you are also forced to relinquish everything that person represented. My husband was a major piece of the total picture I had painted of my life. There were shades of commitment, family, sharing, planning for the future. To let go of him meant letting go of a lifetime of dreams.

What can you do to mop up your tears? Here's some advice on "speed-healing":

● Don't embark on a series of one-night stands to vent your rage, anger, and despair on men in general. Although I have heard this described as a miracle cure, I think it's dicey and usually turns into a tailspin of depression.

● Don't decide you hate everything about yourself, your work, your body, your brains, your looks. This may be a good time for a little cosmetic lift—a few blonde highlights, a weekend at a fancy spa to lose those three or four extra pounds, a splurge on a super dress. The idea of making a fresh start is positive, but don't turn it into a hate-in for yourself. Remember: No one can take away what is yours. Your personality, your abilities, your individuality do not go out the door when the man leaves. You'll hurt, you'll cry for a while, but what's yours is yours. You'll find life does go on, and at another time those special qualities will be appreciated by another man.

• Don't feed your grief by soaking up romantic movies, music, novels, and ballets. Those are for when your heart is full of love, not sorrow.

• Don't concentrate on all the wonderful things he ever said and did. Remember the time he left you waiting in the rain for forty-five minutes or spent the entire party flirting with a woman in a frontless dress or made excuses yet again not to join a family gathering out of town.

• Throw out all the little reminders he so cruelly left behind: his soccer shirt that you slept in on chilly nights, his half-empty bottle of Eau Savage, his soap on a rope. Out, out, out.

• Don't sit home alone, brooding and crying longer than is necessary for that first release from pain. Get out with girlfriends, give a neighborhood brunch, join a club or sports team. Don't mope around encouraging despair and emphasizing your aloneness.

• Don't decide your life is over, that no other man will ever look at you again, so it's okay to eat five pounds of chocolates a night, give up your exercise class, chop your shoulder-length hair into a sensible Buster Brown, and let your mustache grow in! It's always when you've changed from Cinderella into an Ugly Sister that a Greek god moves into the apartment next door or your fuddy-duddy boss is replaced by a Burt Reynolds look-alike.

That's exactly what happened to Jackie. When she broke up with Paul she was utterly destroyed, and what his callousness and infidelity hadn't murdered, she was determined to finish off herself. Overnight she changed from a peppy, well-dressed young woman into a drudge. She slopped around at home and at work until her supervisor told her to smarten herself up a bit: Clients didn't enjoy discussing interest rates with a grim-faced, greasy-haired gnome.

We all thought she'd lose her job, and we were trying to suggest nicely she see a therapist before those all-night, marathon sob-outs blinded her forever when time worked its own therapy. A new salesman appeared in the office. He took a special interest in Jackie and her work, and she responded to his attention (and those honey-brown eyes of his) like a virus to penicillin. One day, in through the door walked the Jackie of old with bouncing hair, blushered cheeks, and glossed lips.

Many women don't snap out of a love depression so fast. No sooner are some over one male monster than they've taken up with another.

Don't you all have friends whom you could beat over the head when they get involved with yet another alcoholic or two-timer or liar? Some women just can't stop picking losers. Why is the only possible man for these women an impossible man?

• If He's Hopeless, Why Do I Hang On?

Numerous therapists came through the studio discussing this one. Basically, many of the women who are repeatedly involved in impossible or dead-end relationships are playing out early childhood patterns and often suffer from low self-esteem. They are desperate for a man's love; any man is better than no man. Love excuses everything in some women's eyes: "As long as he loves me and comes home to me, what do I care if he plays around?" (If he loves you, and that means respecting, liking, and honoring you, too, why does he deliberately wound you? asks Micki.)

"He can't help his drinking. He has a lot of problems." (The Pope, the Queen, your cleaning woman all have problems, and so do I. We solve them, not drink them away. Get your man some help, and if he doesn't want it, get yourself another man.)

"He hit me, but he was beaten as a child, so I understand." (Well, understand this, lady: Hit back. Not with your fists, but with counseling or therapy or some outside help. If it doesn't work, walk out while you can still walk.)

No man (no other *person*) should be allowed to use and abuse you. And they won't be able to if you've got the ammunition we talked about earlier: inner strength, self-esteem, and confidence.

Choosing the same impossible man over and over again is a problem in itself. It's you who needs help as much as he does. Getting it, either by plumbing your own soul for strength and courage or seeking it through a professional, is an investment in your future happiness.

A woman producer whom I worked with on many TV commercials finally saw it this way: "I was always thinking, 'I can't give him up, I need a man.' Then I started thinking that, more than a man, I needed to be happy. I looked back over the last five years and realized how much of it I'd spent depressed or crying. I stopped thinking about a man and pursued happiness as a goal instead. It really worked, because I found I was happier without him and others like him. I've found a different type of man, and I'm content in a relationship for the first time."

How can you recognize one of these impossible men before he moves in? (Or before you fall so hard for him you won't believe he's really impossible and you think you can change him: a trap more dangerous than quicksand.)

There are signs:

• He comes on too strong too soon. He falls madly in love with you instantly; you're the answer to all his dreams.
• His behavior is erratic, even mysterious.
• He confuses you. He swears eternal love and adoration but doesn't call for two weeks.

- He behaves embarrassingly, selfishly, badly with others.
- He drinks excessively.
- His history with women is like Henry VIII's: Use 'em, abuse 'em, dispose of them. (You, honeychild, won't be any different, no matter how hard that is to swallow.)
- He's so in love with himself that he's looking for a groupie or a disciple, not a woman of worth and character. (That's you, remember?)
- He warns you himself: This is the biggie. When a man tells you he's no good, believe him.

- **Can You Trust Another Man?**

Of course. But first you have to trust yourself.

Why should you trust yourself, you, the dummy who's wracked up four chronic cheaters, one married man, two boozers, and a pathological liar?

Because they're all in your past, right?

From today you look at men as people, and they fall into two categories: those you like, with habits and personalities that appeal to you, and those you don't like, with unsavory, unhealthy, downright dangerous habits—like flinging beer bottles at your Sassooned head.

It isn't easy to believe you have the judgment, the control, the common sense to see anyone in a clear light after you've been mixed up with a loser or after a good relationship has folded for whatever reason.

It took me years to fully trust anyone after my marriage collapsed. If I couldn't believe in the golden fairy tale from my youth, what could I believe in? The answer: myself.

By trusting myself I could afford to trust someone else. Actually, Leonard taught me a lot about trust by being trustworthy. He stands by his word.

It's up to you to find a man you can trust, but I can tell you how I started.

When I launched into singledom, I surrounded my-self with trustworthy people: close friends, kind neighbors, good people. Just being with them, I absorbed something of what it is to be "trustworthy." Some of their characteristics I recognized in the men I met, and I began to see that they too were capable of exchanging trust. It also made it easier to recognize the untrustworthiness of rakish, exciting Don Juans who sweep you off your feet but leave you sitting on your fanny in the dawn light, alone.

There's a lot to be worked through for the wounded woman: anger, hostility, resentment at being duped and deceived and dumped and downright crushed. But you can work it through even if you have been jilted in front of a thousand people in an open-air ceremony with three massed bands on live television!

Once you realize it's him, not you, who's lacking, your trampled-down little buds of trust will start to sprout again.

After reading this you might conclude that there are nothing but wolves, sharks, and snakes out there waiting for women, but I know this isn't true. There are plenty of loving, caring, kind, understanding men who would love to have a woman like you—once you really believe in the kind of woman you are.

• *Friends and Lovers—The Fine Line*

I heard a definition of friendship that ran: "Friendship is an acceptance so large it contains everything—the bad and the good."

How many could describe their love relationship like that?

In the best of all possible worlds, friendship is part of love, and love is certainly part of friendship. Yet feelings divide. We are friends with people we couldn't possibly be lovers with, and we sometimes "love" those in a hot, physical sense whom we'd never describe as friends. We barely like them, and we wouldn't tolerate

168

their shortcomings in the long haul.

In the most lasting relationships lovers have to become friends, because the initial fiery passion of love eventually simmers, and the love that is left—a kind of loving friendship—is solid, strong, and primal. And built to last. It's based on the relationship between you as whole people, not just the physical relationship.

Women (and men) who are lonely fantasize about the hottest, sexiest, craziest physical passions. Sex seems to answer every longing. But it is the deeper, truer affection and caring of friendship that drives out loneliness.

I recall a recently divorced man, lonely, craving female company, who went after sexual encounters like a dog chases a cat, because he thought they'd fill his need.

But he felt, he told me, "Like I have the emotional life of a traveling salesman." He felt emptier than ever.

"The next woman I took out, I kissed good night at the door," he said. "I felt like a schoolboy, but I felt good about it. I talked to her, got to know her, got to like her before we went to bed. I still see her, and we have a loving relationship that pleases us both. I've had it with those physical-only encounters."

The early feminist, Mary Wollstonecraft, said, "Love is by it's very nature transitory. The most holy bond in society is friendship."

I don't think she meant love doesn't last. It does. But it transforms itself into another shape and state that has a strong element of friendship in it.

This deep friendship between men and women is not a natural follow-up from the hard-hitting affair, even if the affair leads to marriage. A lot of married folk are not friends.

Men don't make friends the way women do.

Women's friendships arise out of shared feelings, the need for nurturing and support and confiding the contents of our hearts.

Men's friendships are based on shared interests and

activities: fishing, baseball, golf. They don't sit around and talk about their feelings, their fears, their vulnerability. Men don't share that part of themselves and usually do everything under the sun to hide it—from their women and especially from their buddies.

"I can't tell the guys I cried all the way through *E.T.*," a man snorts. "They'll think I'm weird."

Men have a built-in dread of expressing emotion in case they're labeled weak, sissy, or inadequate. Women are helping them open up, but you have to know the man and have a special relationship with him first. A first date is not the time to get out your emotional crowbar and try to pry open the secrets of his heart!

The men I've cared for most in my life are the ones who were confident enough, strong enough, assured enough to say, "This hurts. I'm frightened. Help me." They're tough enough to be soft.

This vulnerability is enormously appealing to women (at least, it is to me), but if your man is afraid of being branded "Coward of the County," start by just offering support and sympathy when you sense he needs it. Don't give up, though. Even John Wayne must have shed a tear once in his life, even if it was only when his horse died!

Now we've disposed of Cupid and his entourage, let's get to Pan and all his lovely lust.

Has anything been so talked about, examined, argued about, disapproved of, celebrated, reveled in, repressed, rejoiced over, battened down, worshipped, and wrangled over as sex?

And there's lots more to say . . . follow me.

VII

Sex

• The Rules You Follow Are Your Own

You have all the rules of sex carved into your bedpost or embroidered on a sampler over the vibrating bean-bag chair, right? Kiss on a first date, cuddle on the second, give in on the third, right? Or hop into bed on the first date because you're liberated. Or don't hop into bed on a first date because you're liberated. Do if he's rich. Don't until he puts that glittering diamond on your finger. You can do it on Tuesdays, Thursdays, and Saturdays, but only if there's a full moon, right? Might as well be, because it's as "right" as any of these rules.

Sex is the most intimate, loving, all-encompassing expression of passion between two people: Don't mess it up with rule-by-committee.

Your sexual code of behavior is the one you can live with, the one that suits your personality and fits in with your lifestyle, beliefs, and ethics.

Other people may have a different set of rules that conflicts with yours: Wish them well and let them follow them. Sex is personal, intimate, and private—and so are the rules that govern it.

Erica, our local brunch organizer who was divorced the same time I was, spent her post-divorce year playing musical men. She loved it! "I felt like I was pigging out on all those lovely men," she confessed. "I went through them like peanuts. It didn't seem to matter. After being married to Joe for ten years I was restless, crazy with boredom and frustration, and I had a great year. I don't regret it. You should try it.''

I shouldn't. I'm glad she enjoyed her twelve-month free-for-all, but me? Me, I need the courtship and romance, and, besides, I don't have the strength to keep changing the sheets!

But neither could I live like my disapproving colleague, Ruth, who was downright shocked when her widowed aunt took a holiday with a man she wasn't married to. Ruth's rules—no sex before marriage under any circumstances—won't work for me, either.

The only rules that suit me are the ones I've tailored to my own desires. They suit my needs for affection, friendship, honesty, gratification, responsibility, pleasure, and happiness.

So I'm not setting rules for you—except the rule of making your own. Trying to follow mine or your mother's or your best friend's or the latest commandments of a woman's magazine could eventually make you feel confused and unhappy if they go against your grain. Your own self-respect and sense of worth will tell you how far you can go in what direction and still smile at yourself in the mirror. Growing up in the 1950s, there were hard and fast rules about sex: Girls who did it were tramps; girls who didn't got the best husbands.

Let me tell you, after years of waiting to experience it, after doing everything but it, after dreaming and talking and wondering about it at countless pajama parties—on my wedding night I couldn't believe this was it!?!?!? This? Whoever said Niagara Falls is the bride's second biggest disappointment of the honeymoon knew what they were talking about!

We all have sets of rules programmed into us from childhood—from parents, the clergy, peers, and the movies. (The Rita Hayworth in me wanted to say, "Yes, yes, yes," but the Doris Day in me emphatically said, "No, no, no.") You have to choose from all of this input what is right for you. Watch out for well-meaning friends and relatives who try to impose their moral judgments on you. Frequently they speak from a comfortable, cocooned, married world and have little understanding of what it means to be single. I say: Be your own judge and do what makes you feel good about yourself.

(By the way, Lisa, this doesn't mean you!!)

Speaking of Lisa and rules, I stopped years ago trying to give her the standard parent's rulebook on boys and dating. I stopped telling her, "Just don't do anything," and "Watch out; boys want only one thing," and all those other speeches parents make to deaf ears. Instead, I've told her that she must put a high value on herself and not give herself away easily in any sense—physically, mentally, or emotionally.

If she (and you) like and respect yourselves, you'll do okay in this wicked world.

Sex is the one area where parents still choke and splutter and clam up in front of their kids. We give them guidance about cars, school, careers, and health—but mention sex, and we freeze. The most mature and open parents turn into Victorian dungeon-keepers at the merest whisper of the birds and the bees.

Personally, I don't think it's a wonderful thing for very young people to indulge in sex. The depths of passion are heady. Adolescence is such a turbulent time that more emotional imbalance can be overwhelming, not to mention the possible life-determining consequences. Statistics, however, keep proving that no one is listening to this one little "rule-ette" of mine, anyway.

One last piece of advice about sex before you turn off the light: Don't be pressured into sex or frightened out of it. It's your body and your spirit that's about to be messed with: Make sure you welcome it. As my friend Alara said, "When a man penetrates my body, he penetrates my mind. I've tried to separate the two, but I can't."

It's not just your body that's involved, but your heart

and soul, so make sure they all agree about what's right for you.

• Don't Trade Sex for Stroking

Some wise woman once said (or cried or shrieked) that men offer intimacy to get sex, and women offer sex to get intimacy. There's some truth in that. Sex, even the most casual, quickie, standing-up-in-the-broom-closet kind, forms a bond between the partners.

The search for that bond (not the sixty-second, but the sixty-year kind) governs our lives.

"When I'm in bed with a man I feel loved and wanted," says one young woman. "Having sex isn't that important to me, but being held is."

My manicurist, a bright, lively sparkler, sometimes spends the night with her former long-time boyfriend. "Richard and I dated for eight years," she says. "We were so close; there is still an emotional tie between us. When either one of us is feeling empty, lonely, or sad, we call the other up and spend the night together, just cuddling and holding each other. Even though we are no longer sexually involved, we still want that comforting touch."

Women need that cuddling, that stroking, and they frequently offer sex to men in the hopes of getting it. If you're offering sex when what you really want is human contact, your problem will not be solved by self-deluding one-night stands.

Rollo May, in his book *Love and Will*, says, "For human beings the most powerful need is not for sex per se, but for relationship, intimacy, acceptance, and affirmation."

I'd say no sex until you get the stroking. That means getting to know someone slowly, gently, caringly. Some people share their bodies more easily than they share their hopes, fears, and aspirations. Be sure you know what you want.

• *Casual Sex: Too Much, Too Soon?*

Most women have met up with a Bedroom Cowboy:
you know, a notch in his Harvey Woods for every
woman he's had. Some women have been B.C.'s themselves, notching their conquests into the waistbands of
their Calvin Kleins.

I never know how to react to these creatures, because
their bedroom pattern isn't mine—but I'm fascinated
with theirs. Fast, easy, casual sex has a whiff of deli-
cious novelty about it. It's wicked, it's forbidden, and it
promises to be more exciting than a regular relationship. It flourishes on holidays, at wild parties, and on
out-of-town business trips—anywhere where the lack
of ties, lack of commitment, and impossibility of in-
volvement combine to produce a fling.

It's just for fun. I'm all for having fun, but I'm also an
incurable romantic. One-night "affairettes" have little
allure for me. I want a total experience—a complete
symphony, not a tune played on a harmonica.

Sex for me doesn't start in bed. It begins with the
anticipation of my lover's arrival, a romantic dinner,
music, flowers, sweet nothings. I want the air to throb
with promise. All that is a little hard to put together on
a one-night stand. I'd rather have a slow waltz than the
last tango in Paris, but I've been told by indulging
women that recreational sex beats a night on the squash
court hands down!

Someone once said to Woody Allen in all seriousness,
"Sex without love is an empty experience."

"You're right," replied Woody. "But as empty experiences go, it's one of the best."

My friend Liz would agree. "I indulged in casual sex
for about six months after my separation. The last year
of our marriage had been sexless, and I came out of it
feeling frigid and undesirable. It was reassuring to find
out that so many men wanted me. I rediscovered my
own sexuality and learned a lot about men. I wouldn't

recommend it as a steady lifestyle, but it was one very important stage of my life."

I wouldn't lecture women who enjoy casual sex, but I wouldn't push it on anyone, either. Sex is a beautiful, fulfilling experience that can turn ugly and demeaning very quickly. You know how best you feel about pleasure and commitment and about what you want and need from a man at this stage of your life. Whatever it is, enjoy it; if you like yourself afterwards, it's for you.

• *Living with a Body You Like*

Marlene tells one of the best stories about "body crisis." She had finally, after months of flirting and a few casual dates, snagged one of the men of her dreams into a romantic dinner à deux at her place.

The evening was going perfectly, and it became obvious that Mr. Wonderful was going to sweep her into his arms and take her Tarzan-like into the bedroom. As she snuggled closer to him, she caught a glimpse down her décolletage of her tummy, a little too full of snails, Chicken Kiev, and wine, and puffed out over her lacy black panties.

Says Marlene: "In that instant I hated my body. I'm so self-conscious about my middle anyway that I was mortified and would have died rather than let him see it. I couldn't have taken my clothes off for anybody at that moment, not even a doctor." She faked instant food poisoning, and he left bewildered!

"It's no good," Marlene says. "If I feel embarrassed by my shape, if I hate my pot belly and realize I should have done those 150 sit-ups a day, I can't feel sexy. I want to hide under the covers with the lights out. I'd rather say no with my clothes on in case he says no when they come off! When my thighs are firm and my tummy is flat, I feel sexier, more confident."

Of course, that's just one definition of sexy. A loving, turned-on man can make you feel sexy about a squint and a mustache!

"I used to think of myself as fat," sighs Maureen. "But Tony went wild the first night we made love. He kept telling me my body was so voluptuous that I was like a big, rich chocolate cake! And his actions matched his words. As long as he thinks I'm sexy, even though I'm not Twiggy, I'm happy. Actually, for the first time I can walk around naked in front of a man without feeling self-conscious. I feel—well, voluptuous."

Men love many things about women's bodies that women hate. I know men who go wild over women who don't shave their underarms. A woman who spent years feeling ugly about her tiny breasts told me she was now with a man who thought they were gorgeous. He called them his precious plums and loved caressing them. (She then decided that they were okay.) Men love chubby thighs (like creamy eighteenth-century goddesses in those naughty paintings), rounded tummies (a sign of fertility—very primal), crooked toes, knock-knees, breasts that could be supported by tape, and breasts that would fill Dolly Parton's tank top. The problem is that women can't love these various "hideousnesses" until a man does.

There's no denying that if you feel uncomfortable, awkward, and self-conscious about your body, your sex life will be affected. If you feel you could have better sex if only you had a better body, then before you get into bed, get into the gym! You can't make legs grow three inches, but you can make those "shorties" firm and tight and nicely defined. You can't have an Amazonian shape if nature made you a Munchkin, but you can be slim and fit.

Exercise is one half; diet is the other. You know that eating an apple, an orange, or a slice of cheese is better for you than a slab of Black Forest cake. There are hundreds of diet books and clinics to get you started and plenty of exercise classes to help you achieve that new shapely, sexy you.

Or perhaps you're like many women: You're not model-shaped, but you're happy. We're talking about fixing a happiness problem here, not creating a perfect physical specimen. There are plenty of gorgeous women with dreadful sex lives, and God knows they've got the equipment to succeed.

This brings me to the most important point: Your biggest erogenous zone is between your ears; it's all in your head. If you can step out of the shower at 180 pounds and feel like Venus rising from the half-shell as your lover swoons with lust—it's up to you whether you want to sweat it out on a gym mat. But if you are unhappy and feel like Sophie Tucker breaking the Brooklyn Bridge, I'd say it's time for serious body toning!

Part of liking your body is knowing your body. Women have picked up the idea (and many men, too) that the sexual parts of a woman are dark, unappealing, and distasteful to the senses; but women should realize that their genitals are beautiful in the same way a sea shell is, or coral, or an intricate flower and that their natural body odors can be erotic. It helps if a woman can talk intelligently to her lover about her body parts, especially if she's asking for some special attention. A man told me he nearly fell out of bed laughing when his partner described her vulva as her volvo. You don't need a course in auto mechanics (or anatomy, for that matter) just to learn the terminology.

• Sexual Power: It Can Be Yours for the Asking

When I was in university there was a pleasant but plain woman in one class called Sarah. She wore little make-up, had unexceptional eyes, and dressed modestly.

But she was surrounded by men. She had a date every weekend; the phone was always for her; males, from professors to freshies, were attracted to her like bees to honey.

We naive gals spending all our spare cash on new clothes and trying every new hairdo and makeup color

178

could never understand it. Sarah wasn't attractive in the usual sense, yet she attracted men. It was as if she wove a magical spell around them.

We could never figure out what her secret was. Now older and wiser, I think I understand why some women like Sarah have that power to attract and hold men. The whole issue of sexual power used to confuse me, because I grew up during a time when a woman's sexuality was used to manipulate men. Often powerless outside the home, women bartered sex in exchange for security, love, status, and material gain. Their sexual allure was enhanced by such things as tight sweaters, revealing décolletage, and spiked heels. Lana Turner herself described it as "flesh impact," a kind of tantalizing sexual promise, appearing receptive but unavailable. Ask any man about the magnetic force of wanting what you cannot have.

For some people this dynamic hasn't changed; stereotypes die hard. But now that women are in a position to negotiate for themselves in the world and don't have to do it through a man, the sexual transaction between men and women has changed.

Sexual power now has a different base. It comes from confidence and self-assurance, from feeling comfortable about sex, about your body, and about yourself. There is an openness, a come-hitherness that radiates from the sensual woman. Not to be confused with French perfume or lace garter belts, it is expressed in her eyes, her voice, her body movements, and her gestures.

These sensual women genuinely like men. They view them not as alien creatures from another planet (reacting with fear, hostility, and misunderstanding), but as individuals worth knowing and enjoying. It comes down to enjoying sex because you love yourself and your man, and your passion colors everything you do. He can see it in the way you run up the stairs or laugh and argue at an auction sale, in the exuberance of your

179

tennis swing, and the way you move to music. Your passion for love is reflected in your day-to-day passion for life: for work and play, for food, music, people—all of life.

The mystery of sexual power is that when it lasts, it becomes a deeper, richer intimacy that involves whole personalities.

• Sexual Fantasies: A Little Spice Is Nice

Fantasies can enliven and enrich your sexual relationship. Some people's fantasies are in technicolor and Dolby sound; they're detailed and frankly fantastic. You wouldn't believe what you can do dressed up like Marie Antoinette or what happens when you're held captive by triplets who look like Placido Domingo! Since you have them, you may as well enjoy them. Don't blush! Share them and act them out!

As long as you and your partner agree on what makes sex "sexy," nothing is wrong, kinky, perverted, or bad. Some people argue that that's what's wrong with sex these days. Nothing's hidden anymore; everything's out in the open and acceptable. Gone are the old taboos, the naughtiness, the tantalizing sense of wickedness. Comedian Lily Tomlin laments, "I remember the old days when the air was clean and sex was dirty."

I was once at the house of a television producer and his live-in girlfriend. Over their bed were two mirrors, both at provocative angles. I'm not sure I'd want to know about the scar, the birthmark, and the tattoo on my lover's behind right at that moment, but if you do, you could be Alice-through-the-Looking-Glass, too!

Having fantasies is normal, healthy, and creative. Ask any sex therapist. Better yet, ask any satisfied lover!

The week before I had tennis ace John Newcombe on the show, I dreamed about him every night. When he was in the guest seat, I told him I'd been dreaming about him. "I've heard that before, Micki," he said.

"Women just want to mother me." "John," I said, "mothering was not what I had in mind."

The ultimate fantasy for some is to act out their fantasies.

Margaret Trudeau said that when she was weathering a storm of criticism over her Hollywood escapades, she wondered how many housewives had dreamed of going to bed with the mailman because he looked like Ryan O'Neal. "Well, I went to bed with Ryan O'Neal," Maggie said. "I lived the fantasy."

Most of us don't cross that line. Fantasies are just that—make-believe stuff. One American study revealed that the average person has up to eight fantasies a day and that homosexual and forced-sex fantasies are common, as are fantasies of group sex and voyeurism. As long as they don't take over and become your sex life, fantasies can prop up your relationship, inspire you, and arouse you.

They may also tell you something about you and your sex life. If you fantasize about being tied up and having Marlon Brando force himself on you, maybe your gentle, laid-back lover should Tarzan it up a bit. Don't be shy—share your fantasy so he'll get the message.

Flagging romances are perked up by shared fantasy. A friend of mine confessed she had always had a swept-off-her-feet fantasy, and always in costume. She and a playful new lover rented nineteenth-century attire—a pretty Empire-waist ballgown for her, full military rig for him—and acted out her dream attack. He chased her up the staircase, and (how unfortunate!) she stumbled at the top! He caught her ankle and forced her to the floor! She struggled but to no avail! He had his wicked way with her! "It was the most thrilling night of my life," she says. And the costumes were only slightly ripped.

When asked if he thought sex was dirty, Woody Allen replied, "It is if you do it right."

• Sexual Criticism: How's Your Bedside Manner?

Sex is perfectly natural but not naturally perfect.

Just because you're both madly in love, insane with lust, and jumping on each other all day like kangaroos doesn't guarantee that every second is bliss.

We have all met the man who hates to kiss although he loves to be kissed, the man who won't believe that having your back rubbed is a sexual turnon, the man who wants you to do 101 things to him but he's not getting experimental with you, the man who thinks orgasm should be a race like the Grand Prix, and the man who thinks that what worked for his first wife will work just as well for his second.

Of course, if you listen to men you hear the stories in reverse. There's the woman who refuses to touch his penis, the one who wants the whole sex act over as quickly as possible (she should get together with the Grand Prix racer), the one who doesn't like anything except the missionary position, and the one who likes everything except the missionary position. There's the woman who wakes him at four a.m. to do it again when he's worried sick about a big sales meeting at eight and the woman who insists on doing it in the bath, even though there's no room for two large people and he's scraped the skin off his knees and elbows twice.

When you start cataloging the complaints and criticisms, it's a wonder people don't stay home and collect butterflies instead!

A dear aunt gave me this piece of advice before marriage: "Whatever he wants to do in bed, let him. It's his right. Tell him he's wonderful. It's your duty." Times have changed; we no longer lie there and think of England. Lovers can criticize each other if they do it in the way they do everything together: lovingly, caringly, and honestly. This doesn't mean yelling: "Ouch, you big gorilla—get your elbow out of my eye!" or: "For God's sake, Gloria, show some emotion—I feel like a necromaniac!"

Well, what should you say? How should you handle this? The important thing is never to belittle him or make him feel stupid or inadequate.

Perhaps your lover is inexperienced. Maybe he doesn't know how much gentle (or not-so-gentle) foreplay a woman requires to match his level of arousal. Sometimes in their eagerness men head for the bed with the same attitude they have when they head for the baseball diamond: "Forget the warm-up. Let's play ball." Maybe he's shy or fighting a stereotype of what he thinks all women want in bed.

Talk to him; show him gently what to do. You don't have to put the light on, reach for the sex manual, and read page 49 aloud for him to get the message. "Mm, that feels nice," you might say, "but this feels even better." Or: "That's good, but will you try it like this, too?" He'll get the message. After all, he loves you and is trying to please you.

Don't come on like a drill sergeant or a theater critic. Emphasize the positive and gently express what you want. Otherwise, something else will start to droop along with his sensitive ego, and you'll be spending nights with the light on reading the sex manual—alone.

One day it might be you on the end of the sexual criticism stick. A man might tell you you aren't doing something right. "Oh well," you might sniff, "it was good enough for Clive . . ." A better reaction would be, "Show me, then, show me how to pleasure you."

This reaction led Lynda, a newly divorced woman, into fresh flights of fancy with her new lover. He showed her what he wanted. She was fascinated watching him masturbate, and he got super turned-on with her watching with such lust in her eyes. Before they knew it, they'd invented a whole new love game. Now that's constructive criticism.

One rule applies to both sexes: Never, on pain of being celibate for the rest of your life, criticize physical attributes or compare your lover with a lover of the past.

One thing that leads lovers to criticism is sexual boredom. Maybe the affair or marriage just doesn't have the same zip it did six months ago.

Before you start blaming your lover, take some responsibility yourself for jazzing things up. The components of a sexual relationship are not just he-she. They're also time, place, attire. Surprise him by lying naked on the couch surrounded by flowers when he comes home! Jump in the shower with him and make him late for work! Go to the drive-in and reenact your teenage fantasies. Wear a leopard-skin bikini and crack the whip! I don't know what you have to do, but you will. When you've exhausted your repertoire he will undoubtedly come up with some surprises of his own.

• Is There Lust after Marriage?

An old joke runs like this: The parson asks the woman of the house if her husband believes in life after death. Wistfully she replies, "He doesn't even believe in life after dinner." Do I hear a round of applause from the wives and long-time lovers out there? Do we have to take for granted that lovemaking means lights out, missionary position, after the news? It becomes so predictable and passionless.

Folks who live together can get into rigid patterns: same conversations, same routines, same responsibilities, same sex life. It's hard to see the woman with dust and floor wax and baby sick-up on her overalls as a seductive creature, waiting to go wild in the sack; but under that household debris is the raven-haired temptress who once insisted on doing it on the observation deck of the CN Tower. And him—beneath those baggy jeans and paint-splattered undershirt lurks the man who insisted, between mouthfuls of strawberries and champagne, on having his way under the dining room table at your sister's wedding with five hundred guests in the next room!

Can we find those lustful, beautiful creatures again? I

think so. Variety, atmosphere, and time can go a long way to rekindling desire.

First, where to make love. Forget the bedroom. Like Mount Everest, it's always there. Here's a wonderful list of new (or maybe, to worldly exciting you, not so new) places culled from friends who are more naughty than nice:

- In an elevator.
- On the balcony.
- In a whirlpool bath.
- In the back seat of a car in a lover's lane.
- In a sauna.
- In a hammock.
- In the doctor's office—if your man is the doctor.
- On an airplane, under a blanket, over the Atlantic.
- In a cubbyhole at the Tower of London. (Watch out for Anne Boleyn's ghost!)
- On the sheepskin rug in front of the fireplace.
- In a sleeping bag in a starry forest.
- In a rocking chair.
- In a straw-filled stable.
- In the cloakroom of a large metropolitan art gallery.
- Backstage at the theater during intermission.

And here's one of my favorites:

- In the change room of an exclusive menswear store while the manager keeps asking at the door if everything fits all right!

Now that we've changed the place, what about the time? Forget the night. Meet your man for "funch" at a glitzy hotel or, better yet, a ratty motel. Or meet in an underground parking lot (very dark and private in the car) at midday. Set the clock ahead an hour—you'll discover a part of his body gets up before he does. Or how about weekend afternoons (ship the kids to granny's) or the middle of the night while he's still asleep. Start gently, persuasively—he'll wake up to such a lovely surprise.

Sometimes what's missing from long-term sex isn't the excitement, but the tenderness. Dina says, "He used to touch my face, stroke my shoulders, and rub my back—now it's just straight down to business. I miss the gentleness we used to share."

So much of what is missing in these relationships is easy to put back just by putting it back. Start touching his face again (or hers), or take your partner's hand and put it on your face (or wherever you want it)—he'll remember. He may be surprised, but he'll be touched that you still want him in the same passionate way. Being wanted is a powerful aphrodisiac.

If the passion has gone out of your marriage, consider this: Whatever happens in bed at night between partners is an extension of what happens to them during the day. If the scenario starts with arguments over money, kids, or business pressures, don't expect it to end with "a hot time in the old town tonight." If, however, at the end of a busy day you both take time to unwind, communicate, and share what has to be done, the scene is better set for romance. Marriage should mean a license to explore, not bore.

• *Sexual Inhibitors: Do You Have Any?*

Men and women have some in common, but each person has a secret vault where the most uncomfortable and unacknowledged inhibitions are locked away.

For her these are some sexual inhibitors. One or all of these can interfere with a healthy sex drive:

• Sex is dirty; it's something only bad girls and tramps enjoy.
• Most sex acts are dirty. The missionary position with your eyes shut is okay, but anything else is suspect.
• My body isn't firm enough, young enough, and doesn't smell good enough.

- I'm afraid to make the first move in case he thinks I'm cheap or aggressive.
- I'm afraid of not having an orgasm.
- I'm afraid of not having multiple orgasms.
- I'm afraid of not having extended orgasms.
- I'm afraid of not being as good/talented/beautiful as the last woman he slept with.
- How will he react if I know too much in bed?
- He won't respect me in the morning.

For him:

- I'm afraid of not being able to perform, or losing my erection, or not getting one in the first place.
- I'm afraid my penis is too small.
- I'm afraid I won't be able to bring her to orgasm—single, multiple, extended, or any kind.
- I'm afraid of premature ejaculation.
- I'm afraid of being impotent.
- I'm afraid of not being as good/talented/handsome as the last man she went to bed with.

One of the most common fantasies for men is the myth of unlimited sexual prowess. Men search for it like the Holy Grail. When I interviewed one author of the book on the G spot, she advised women that they could enhance their lovemaking by "kegeling" exercises. How can I explain this to you without getting too graphic? It's kind of like yodeling, but with a different part of your body.

Then she went a step further and suggested kegeling for men. "How," I asked, "do men kegel?"

"Well," she said, "men take a warm washcloth, fold it four times, and drape it over the end of an erect penis. Then the man slowly raises and lowers it to a count of four."

There was a deathly silence—remember, we're on live TV—which I finally broke by chirping, "If he gets really good he can join the circus!" After the show one of the crew members, a big, strapping, macho guy, came over and whispered in my ear, "I don't use a washcloth; I use a bucket of sand!"

Anyone suffering from sexual anxiety to the point that they avoid sex altogether or can't enjoy it should start reading some of the self-help books on the market. Talk to your partner about it. If necessary, consult a therapist.

Micki says to women that the only thing dirty about sex is the language, sometimes, if you get off on talking dirty. That your body is just fine, or he wouldn't be in bed with you in the first place. That making the first move is one of the sexiest and most stimulating things you can do for a man. That having an orgasm is not the goal of sex: Orgasm is a lovely bonus, but not a necessity, and anyone sexually knowledgeable can have one. If you don't have the knowledge, back to the books and the therapists.

I'll talk to the men, too.

Losing an erection is okay as long as you've also lost your heart and the woman knows it. Love conquers all!

Let's put this issue of penis size to rest once and for all. According to Dr. Joyce Brothers, the average penis is four inches long; in it's full glory it's six. I have never, ever heard women express concern over the size of a man's penis. It seems to be a male hang-up.

Lovemaking is a shared experience, not a competitive event. There are no judges and no points for performance.

And about premature ejaculation: She may be flattered you were so excited.

For both sexes, the first inhibition that must be overcome is the inhibition to communicate. Talk to each other!

Now, just a word about differences in attitudes toward sex, because they often result in sexual inhibitions. Men and women make love differently. Women usually need and prefer more kissing and touching than men. A study showed that in a matter of 120 seconds, a man could be aroused and reach orgasm. It took women an average of twenty minutes to complete the arousal-to-orgasm cycle. That's a gap of eighteen minutes to fill with foreplay, loving words, and caresses. It's nice, but it isn't as necessary for a man.

Men find it easier to see sex as a purely physical release. They can separate "making love" from "having sex." The latter, as one man once told me, is like a good game of handball.

Men are more aroused by visual stimulation than women. Men get erections just looking at the nubile nymphs in *Penthouse*. Women might look at nude men in *Playgirl*, but they rarely get aroused by them. They're more likely to get turned on by the whole man, his style of dress, his thick, wavy hair, his cologne.

Men seem to want more sex; women want better sex.

Since men and women are so different and often have difficulty understanding each other, it's amazing that anyone gets together under the covers at all. But we do!

• Celibacy: Is There Bliss without Sex?

What a medieval word, conjuring up images of monks and virgins locked in towers. Not at all! In the midst of the sexual revolution, celibacy has gained a respectable foothold. It can revitalize the soul!

Charlotte elaborates: "Since I gave up sex I feel more energetic. My mind's clearer; I'm more content. I was tired of my own patterns, of hopping into bed with every new man, of all those inevitable separations, of not being able to say no. Well, now I've said it, and I feel refreshed." But Charlotte's "No" isn't forever.

"When I meet a man I like and care for, I'd love to make love again," she says.

Margo, who is also celibate, adds that since forswearing men, she's become more attractive to them. "I think it's because I'm calm, not looking, not anxious," she says. "I'm friendlier and more open. I'm not playing any games. Men are interested in me now as a person, not just a potential sexual partner."

Of course, some embittered women decide to be celibate because they've got such a rotten deal from men in the past that they can't stand the pain of rejection any more. In this case choosing celibacy is simply avoiding the problem of their hostility toward men. If you opt for celibacy, check your motives. Make sure you see it as a positive option that will redirect and reenergize you.

• *Getting What You Want in Bed*

After all this talk about sex, do you really know what you want in bed?

It's easy to make a list of what you *don't* want—cracker crumbs, belching, snoring, sixty-second quickies, and Dracula's brother. But what about what you do want? Do any of these fit your list?

- Someone to care about me.
- Gentleness and tenderness.
- Someone who enjoys sex.
- Creativity and imagination.
- Someone who loves and appreciates my body.
- Someone who appreciates my efforts to please him.
- Excitement and pleasure.
- Someone I can talk to and relax and be spontaneous with.

Everyone has a right to a happy sex life—one that pleases them, makes them feel good about themselves and their partner, fills them with joy and peace, and sends them off to sweet dreams. But be sensible.

During a show on "sexual nutrition," I made the mistake of asking a sexpert about external aphrodisiacs. He advised men to dip their penises in warm milk before sex. "Skim or two per cent?" I asked. And don't get hung up on the ESO (extended sexual orgasm) that's supposed to last thirty minutes! Talk about performance anxiety!

One of the first steps to getting what you want in bed is looking like you're after something. If you hit the sack in an old flannel nightie, with hair in curlers, an inch of cream on your face, and an eye mask, nobody except Boris Karloff's mummy is going to come near you.

Perhaps the most important step is being able to say out loud to him what you want. Many women assume that men magically understand them and know what they need. When they don't get it, they rant and rave and blame the poor guy. He's not a mind reader; you'll have to speak up.

If you're still not satisfied, maybe the place to start looking is outside the bedroom. Sex often follows the path of the entire relationship. A miserable or indifferent one is not going to produce an explosive sex life. Why are you and your beloved spending every night arguing or all weekend in front of the TV? If your sex life is repressive and unhappy, look at the rest of your relationship. Is it the same?

You get what you want in bed in the same way you get what you want from life: by knowing what it is, by considering how best to get it, by knowing you deserve it, and by having the confidence, self-esteem, and good judgment to seek it.

The woman who knows what she wants and pursues it with energy and love will usually find it sleeping blissfully on her pillow in the morning.

And with that thought, good night and sweet dreams!

VIII

Love: Liking, Lusting, Lasting

• Is This the Real Thing?

What in the world is there left to say about love?

Since poets first put pen to paper, hearts and flowers have been pouring out, spilling into countless books, romantic novels, paintings, and music. Everyone from the ancient Greeks to the anonymous scribe who writes those corny greeting card verses has tried to say something original about this craziness that can be the most painful and most joyous of human experiences.

There are as many definitions of love as there are lovers: Love is a vacation from reality (I'd say it makes its own reality); love is what you try hard to find just before the bar closes (too full of angst); love is what makes women shave their legs (and keep their underwear in good repair); the love that lasts the longest is the love that is never returned. (How true! How true!)

Shakespeare said love is madness, and so have half the women I've known! Duels have been fought for it, wars waged for it, hearts (and heads) broken because of it. Lovesick men and women have abandoned their life's work, their families, their honor in the thrall of this demon.

Now that I've scared you off, may I just say: Isn't love wonderful? Life without it is like a plain pudding: nice but uninspiring. Life with love is the richest confection ever set before you, and you want to gobble, gobble, gobble.

But what is it? Let's borrow a bit from love expert Nathaniel Branden and call romantic love a passionate combination of emotional, spiritual, and sexual attachment between a man and a woman, firmly based on respect and admiration. Or, as my friend Ellen says, "It's like having the Milky Way in my head and Niagara Falls pouring through my heart." I never understood her exactly until I fell in love again, and now I agree totally.

Branden also says that true romantic love satisfies our need for human companionship and for shared values and feelings, interests, joys, and burdens. It stretches our need to exercise our emotions to the limit. It satisfies our craving to be nurtured, fulfills our sexual needs, and increases our confidence to see we are admired, loved, and wanted by another human being.

We all spend our lives pursuing it, and yet sometimes those who seem most likely to reap armfuls of love come up empty-handed. I think of Marilyn Monroe, who spent her life searching for the real thing and who, despite her glamour, beauty, success, and fame, said sadly, "I have loved many, but I'm not sure if I've ever been loved."

Without love our lives would be bleaker and thinner, and an important dimension would be missing. Love makes you feel alive—unless, of course, it makes you feel miserable! Like loving the man who doesn't love you back or forgiving him, again, for insulting your family, for not showing up when he was supposed to, for sleeping with your girlfriend, for lying like a triple agent!

Before you let yourself in for all this misery (and/or splendor), how can you tell if it's infatuation or the real thing? Branden (the last time I quote him, honest) believes there is a critical point in a love relationship when it produces a clarity of its own, and suddenly you can see it for what it is. I pray this happens to you if you're in an "I think this is it" situation. If you have to debate, wonder, argue whether this is love, it probably isn't. Being in love is like having a baby. Once the process starts you can't stop it. You can't say to Cupid any more than you can say to Mother Nature: "Hey, wait a minute, I'm not ready. I've got a lot of other things to do right now—catch me later, okay?" Once you're in love you're there, in another country, and whether you stay there happily and prosperously will be determined by the two of you.

People have their own signals and turning points that tell them it's the real thing and they are in love.

"I knew I loved Joel when we were at a performance of the 1812 Overture and I didn't hear the cannons go off."

"I knew it was the real thing with Dennis when it was more important to me to touch him, talk to him, and hold him than go to bed with him."

"I knew this was it with Ron when he introduced me to his parents as the woman he loved. It was the first time I'd met them, he'd never said he loved me, and he chose that moment to announce it! Any man with that much courage and openness is for me."

After all this highfalutin talk I'm almost embarrassed to tell you how I knew I loved Leonard: I sent a chocolate chip cookiegram to him at work with "I Love You" written on it. You can interrupt Leonard at work for a million-dollar deal, but a five-dollar mound of dough? I must have been crazy, but Leonard must have been, too, because instead of scratching my name out of his little black book, he scratched the book. Lovers are permitted any madness.

The hard thing about the real thing is that you may have to go through a few practice runs before you get to it. These practices usually hurt. Sometimes it's a twinge, sometimes a jolt. Sometimes it's like falling off the top of Mount Everest. It won't ease the pain to tell you these are experiences to learn from, but they can be.

The only thing I can promise you is that when you do fall into the real thing, its warmth, its passion, its contentment and goodness will make up for the painful bite of those infatuations that ended badly. So you must promise me not to let them get you so down and swampy with grief that you hide away and never let yourself love again. Real love is worth every breath in your body. Now tack that up on the bathroom mirror and take his picture with all the darts in it down!

• *Choosing a Mate, Not a Date*

I don't know why God decided that mates and dates should be such completely different creatures, but She did! As much as I adored tangoing with Rocco under the stars, I could never have married a man who wore more makeup than I did!

Although Vance's kisses drove me into ecstasy, his habit of sitting around the pool picking his toenails immediately put him on the "forever bachelor" list in my mind.

Even though Pete promised eternal love and showered me with so many flowers the house looked like a funeral parlor, I heard him phoning another woman for a date when I left to make drinks.

These men were great dates, but lousy mates. Who we're looking to play with isn't necessarily who we want to live with. So distinguish early between men who are sexy and fun and as disposable as razor blades and men who are sexy and fun and have the heart you're hunting for!

I knew when I headed into my present serious relationship that I didn't want to be babied and protected, but I did want to feel cherished and cared for. Could any man strike the right balance?

In his own inimitable style, Leonard has found a way. These two stories illustrate our relationship. When the

TV crew from the show were filming me roller-skating down the street, Leonard ran alongside me with his arms stretched out in case I fell, hiding behind every tree and garbage can to avoid the camera until the crew were laughing so hard they couldn't work!

Recently, while vacationing at a northern lodge, I decided to try windsurfing. There I was, being buffeted around on the lake, struggling with the sail but holding my own when over my shoulder who do I see but Leonard calmly paddling along in a canoe—with two lifejackets—all set to rescue me if I capsized and ruined my hair!

That just about sums up his attitude: He'd never stop me from doing anything, but he does what he can to cushion the fall!

Men and women supposedly look for different things in mates. Men, according to Joyce Brothers, are always attracted to beauty first and list attractiveness and sex appeal as "Numero Uno" on millions of dating service file forms. There have been enough studies done on what makes people marry to fill every wedding chapel in North America, but I don't think anyone will ever really know. It's a mix of mystery, magic, practicality, sex, chemistry, love, erotic fantasies, untold dramas, humor, desire, and timing.

Because there are so many variables and love can be so insane, here's a no-no list to consider:

• Don't marry someone you find physically repulsive. ("You have a good heart, Harry, but I don't like your corns.")
• Don't marry someone with a totally different sense of humor than yours and who thinks yours is stupid.
• Don't marry someone who hates children when you want ten.
• Don't marry on the rebound from an unhappy affair. ("I'm sorry, Bill. Did I call you 'Charlie?'")
• Don't marry someone a generation older or younger. (Ask Pierre and Maggie.)

• Don't marry someone with whom you've had great sex but have never really talked.

Doing nothing Saturday night? Make a chart of all the men in your life, list all the characteristics you'd want in an ideal mate, and see who measures up. You can list the characteristics under Absolute Necessities (like kindness, affection, money, humor, loyalty), Pleasant Enough But Can Live Without (moralistic, intelligent, urbane, charming), and No Way (cruel, stingy, unfaithful ... Well, go on, this is your list.) It's an excellent (and fun) way of weeding out the unmarriageable men.

Of course, all this is based on the assumption that you want to be married (or cohabiting). What else are we talking about here but the long, long term? (If you have no interest in being married or are married and have no interests, skip along to the next chapter.) If you really want to be married you must weed men out ruthlessly; end any relationships that you know aren't going anywhere, because you'll need all your time and energy to pursue a marriageable man. (There *are* some out there.)

Make sure you get the man you want to marry, not just the marriage. When I asked Betty after her bitter divorce why she'd married him in the first place, she replied, "Because he's the only one who asked."

There are some men to watch out for and avoid if you're seriously considering matrimony:

• Confirmed bachelors well into their forties with exquisite apartments and routines set in concrete are not good bets. They enjoy being single and are dates, not mates.
• Gay men are gay. No matter how handsome, sexy, witty, what a great cook and charmer he is—what he's after, you ain't got and never will have, so forget it. You won't change him.
• In fact, the object of marriage is not to change people. You must fall in love with your man for who he is

and what he brings out in you, not what you can make him into. He is not a couch to be reupholstered.

• You also will not transform a cruel man into a kind one, a disheveled one into a snappy dresser. Leave the transformation scene to the Princess and the Frog. You're looking for a man who's already together. If he's falling apart you will be, too, before the honeymoon's over.

When you find the man you want to spend your life with, remember: However closely two lovers become entwined, they are still two distinct human beings. Marriage is about two people who love, comfort, support, and respect each other. If you can say all this about your man and your relationship, then maybe you are both ready for the big plunge.

• *Emotional Intimacy: Do You Want It?*

Now we're neck-deep in all this prattle about love, can we consider something momentous here: Do you really want to be in love? What kind of a question is that, you ask indignantly? Everyone wants to be in love.

Yes and no. Some people are frightened of real commitment. Yes, they do if it means they can have it on their own terms, but no, they don't if it means giving themselves away to another person, opening up their deepest secrets, surrendering themselves, and not holding back.

There's an element of ambivalence in most male-female relationships. "I want to get close to you, but I'm afraid to" is the message many people send out. "I love you, but you're driving me crazy" is telegraphed back and forth.

One of the most ambivalent statements of love I've ever seen was in a note Lisa wrote to her brother: "Dear Lance, you are my brother and I love you, but if you forget to pick up the fireworks I will tear your guts out through your nostrils. Love, Lisa."

Love demands an outpouring of trust and honesty; it is a risk that some people find difficult to take.

"My man never talks to me." "He never says what he's really thinking." "We've lived together for three years, but I feel I don't really know him." "He never says how badly he hurts, what bothers him." "He keeps to himself. That's just his way." How often have you heard (or said) these things about a man?

Some women have this problem, too, like a friend who said to me, "Why should I tell Don how badly I need to be held? If he can't see it for himself . . . If I say it to him in words he'll think I'm weak. Then he'll have a way of hurting me." She really said it. But that's what emotional intimacy is: revealing all your idiosyncrasies and fears to your loved one. It's a frightening yet trusting step to take. It creates the kind of unspoken empathy and deep closeness that cement a couple together. On the other hand, it also makes you vulnerable; your loved one has the ammunition to hurt you.

Because of what I know about Leonard there are certain things I would not do or say even as a joke, because I know they would hurt him. He trusts me not to tell anyone, and I trust him not to ridicule my insecurities or tease me about some of my more sensitive spots.

I get so vulnerable when I'm in love that I almost can't get up to face the day in case it's the last one. I can't bear it that my loved one is flying out of town. What if the airplane crashes on takeoff? Or on landing? What if the taxi he gets from the airport is involved in a pileup on the highway? What if the hotel burns down? What if he gets food poisoning in the hotel restaurant? What if some gorgeous nurse gives him mouth-to-mouth resuscitation, and he falls in love and never comes home? Better the plane should crash!

So who in their right mind would want to fall in love? I guess I would, all over again, with the same man. For every ounce of pain it delivers, there comes a pound of pleasure. Emotional intimacy is worth it.

• Building a Loving Relationship

An acquaintance said to me just the other day that she couldn't believe Leonard and I have lived together for some time. "Micki," she said sarcastically, "you were holding hands the other night at that party like it was your first date."

I don't hold hands on a first date, I told her.

Seriously, what is wrong with being romantic with the person you love?

Being affectionate in public, holding hands, touching, exchanging smiles: Do all these things have to be thrown out because you're sharing the same laundry basket? I have seen couples at social gatherings who immediately split up. He heads for his crowd, she for hers. They don't touch, talk, eat, or dance together. I've always wondered what they say to each other on the way home. All of us need to be touched affectionately. And I believe it's one of the building blocks of a loving relationship. Your partner is still your love interest, even when he's half the mortgage and the guy who takes the garbage out—so show it.

Have you got a pencil? Will you please check off how many of these you indulge in or how many you didn't and wish you had now that he's living across the street with someone else.

Couples stay in love because they:

• Express love verbally. You can't say "I love you" too many times if you mean it. If you don't, saying it once is once too many.
• Are affectionate physically. This doesn't mean leaping onto your paramour at the annual company picnic right at the president's feet or dragging him off to the spare bedroom at a party, but whoever got arrested for nuzzling while dancing or kissing a sweet thank-you when

he brings you a glass of wine in a crowded theater lobby?

• Make love. Early and often. And late and often. And often, often, often. The happiest marriages or relationships are those with lots of uninhibited, joyous sex.

• Accept each other's strengths and weaknesses. Love him for what he is, not for what you wish or would like him to be.

• Express admiration, appreciation, and respect for each other. Some people think it's enough to feel it and assume their partner knows. Even though you told him not too long ago, tell him again. He'll glow and grow under praise. Don't you?

• Are there for each other. If this is the day he got fired or had his brilliant idea rejected, he needs solace. So cancel your tennis game, make your excuses to the party hostess. He'll do the same for you one day.

• Tell their mates when something is bothering them. If you keep silent, how can he know? The longer you brood on it, the more of an issue—and a potentially destructive one—it will become. Be honest.

• Create time to be together. Even if it means saying "No" to your kids, your best friends, and responsibilities outside your home, do it. Make the time to talk and laugh unhurriedly together, to make love without pressure, to relish your relationship.

Love needs nourishment to survive and grow. You can't just say, "Well, I'm in love, that's that, what's next in life?" Because love, like life, changes. The heady novelty of the first flush of romantic love will deepen into a mutual trust, interdependency, and a stronger passion.

I've heard men say, as the relationship was crumbling, "I said I loved her—what more does she want?" Some evidence, I suspect. The last time he said he loved her was because she asked, and the time before that was three years ago, when they celebrated their fifth anniversary.

"I've been busy earning a living," he says. "But not a loving," I say. Loving is living and vice versa. Both need all the help they can get. Love is up against job pressures and the brutal realities of taxes and mortgages, dental bills, kids' problems, fatigue, familiarity, family hassles. It is so fragile yet so strong. To make it into an indestructible oak you have to pay genuine attention to the acorns of trust and affection and respect from which it grows.

A friend of mine told me a touching story about a couple who were virtual strangers after their twins arrived. The babies were up day and night; one evening they passed on the stairs as he was coming down to the study to do some work and she was going up to the bawling twins with another bottle. They looked at each other in the gloom, hair rumpled, bags under their eyes that Jackie Onassis could pack, and he said, "Honey, this has been the worst year of our lives. And I love you so much, I'd do it all over again."

Now that is loving kindness!

• *Running from Commitment*

Naturally, reading all this has made you die to get out there and find that loving man. Now, I must add that there are men who will run an Olympic mile from any kind of commitment. You've probably met one. He may like you, lust after you, even say "I love you": But in the crunch he doesn't want to get involved.

Says Sandra, a film editor and divorcée looking for a new commitment, "One of the funniest (now it's over) episodes in my life was with Rick. We had spent a wild weekend in Montreal. We were seeing each other every night, all night. He practically camped out in my apartment. He phoned me six times a day at work, he wrote 'I want you forever' in shaving cream on the shower door, he talked about a ski weekend in the Laurentians. He was like a piece of gum on my shoe I couldn't dislodge.

"Then one day I casually mentioned my sister was here from out of town, would like to meet him, and why didn't he join us for lunch? His face just froze. Meet a member of the family? You should have heard the excuses. When I finally pinned him down he said, 'Sorry, Sandy, I don't want to get involved.' Involved! This was the guy who had shared my bed, my body, my food, my fantasies, good times, and laughs; now meeting a relative was suddenly 'getting involved!' He literally decamped that night. I didn't know that meeting a sister was a signal I was planning a June wedding. It was wild."

Lucky Sandra to take it with such aplomb.

Women complain that men run from commitment like hares from hounds. It's not that women don't, but it appears to be more often and more obvious with men. Anyone who's been hurt is doubly wary when they launch themselves back into the singles scene—"once bitten, twice shy" and all that.

And there is a slew of reasons to keep you sitting alone in your room or chalking up notches on the night table. (The two extremes of fleeing commitment are isolation and promiscuity.) People are frightened to fall in love and make the commitment because:

- They feel they're not lovable.
- They're terrified of rejection.
- They're worried that falling in love will give the other person too much power over them—power to hurt them.
- They believe their partner will sooner or later betray them, and they couldn't stand the pain.
- They're afraid of losing their identity and being swamped by the lover's personality.
- They fear appearing foolish.
- They don't want the responsibility of a home, children, or another person's happiness.
- They don't believe love exists, so why invest time and effort in a make-believe idea?

• They fear happiness. Says Louise, a makeup artist, "I can't relax if I'm happy. I'm afraid to let go and enjoy it, because I think something dreadful is waiting around the corner. I'm always primed and ready for the letdown."

You can usually recognize people who are running from commitment because they have been badly burned: They're slightly sarcastic, even bitter about other people's happiness and suspicious of the world's good nature.

Avoiding commitment does not always come out of fear. There are people who have made a genuine choice not to be committed. Their reasons could be: career, school, financial goals, spiritual activities, travel, or simply preferring the single life. If that's you, tallyho!

• Compromising for Love

Oh, Micki, you moan, I'd love to have a committed relationship, but he is so unreasonable, and I'm not giving up everything, and certainly not this and that, and blah, blah, blah. One of the things that keeps loving couples loving is learning to compromise. Compromise! Now, before you leap into your huffmobile and roar away, let me explain: The days when a woman gave all for love—her career, her identity, her dreams—are as dead and long gone as jousting or traveling by donkey cart.

That isn't compromise, that is living sacrifice.

Compromise means you don't give up yourself, but you might retreat on issues you thought were definite—but only after open, fair discussion with your loved one. (After all, the other half of successful compromise is that he has to give up a few things, too.)

One of Leonard's business associates told me she had had no idea that Rob needed every Saturday off to play squash, that he couldn't tolerate pop music on the stereo for a minute, or that he refused to have pets (even a fish) in the house. Of course, she'd never told him that she'd love to live with him, but only if it was blazing a trail to marriage, that she was allergic to his pure wool carpets, and that she had no intention of cooking.

So how are they doing?

After a year Rob has stopped playing squash Saturdays and plays Thursday nights instead. He accepts Barry Manilow and Chicago in small doses, but there's still no golden Lab or even a Pekinese. Penny, on the other hand, still has not got her diamond ring, sneezes over the carpets, and has never so much as cracked an egg for an omelet: The new housekeeper does that.

No two people, not you and Mother, not you and your best friend or beloved child, and certainly not you and your lover can live under the same roof without making some adjustments. If you go hard heartedly and inflexibly into a relationship saying, "I'm changing nothing, altering not a whit, I can save you the trouble of packing," it won't work. Make the distinction between compromising yourself (your values and standards) and making compromises with your mate for the sake of a smoother life together. For instance, asking you to give up your hobby of photography is ridiculous. Asking you to limit the number of three-month photo shoots to Java with your Tom Selleck look-alike instructor isn't.

Now, the big thing about compromises is that they have to be a bargain between the two of you. You think that's obvious? Not in a lot of relationships. For example, the woman makes a compromise with herself (to please him) and doesn't tell her partner. All right, she says, gritting her teeth, I won't see my friend Beth anymore, and I'll give up these kinky clothes because I know they bug him, but dammit . . .

But she never tells him; she just does it. He probably doesn't even notice, and if he does, he assumes she gave up Beth and the theatrical garb because she saw the light or got bored and is into something else. This doesn't work. She brews and stews and sulks about it, and suddenly, out of the blue, he mentions there's a button missing on his shirt, and she explodes. He doesn't know what she's talking about, and ladies and gentlemen, the nine-round, knock-down, drag-out fight is about to begin. Talk it out and reach the compromises together.

I have made an effort to get to places on time for Leonard (although it kills me). Leonard valiantly struggles to give up making business calls from home in the evening (our time together), because he knows it bugs me. We've talked about it, had a little tiff, and now we're trying. Together. At least we know what the other person wants in order to make the relationship better.

The thing to fix in your brain forever is that relationships change and shift like sand on the shore. Your compromises (all right then, call them adjustments) need to accommodate that, too. Maybe you did promise to give up the six a.m. jog and run after work instead because he was working the graveyard shift and didn't get to bed until four in the morning. Now he's back on days and in the land of the living, you can jog at dawn if you want to. Maybe your allergy to cigar smoke has finally cleared up, and he could now light up the smelly things in the dining room instead of being banished to the back porch. Even the best of lovers have to find some middle ground to get on with the daily business of living in the world.

Commitment is glorious, but like everything worthy and worthwhile it has its price. If you consider not being allowed to hang your pantyhose from the shower rod as an infringement of your personal space instead of a reasonable request not to have to fight through a nylon sea of octopus legs to get to the john, maybe you should rethink the idea of sharing the same house.

With compromise, as with every important deal you negotiate in life, the trick is knowing how much you can afford to pay, what the bottom line really is, and when it's the best time to get value for money—even when you're paying in kisses!

● *Romantic Malnutrition: Finding the Remedy*

You love each other so much, but the fire is dying down just the same.

You meant to tell him you loved what he did last night, but you're already late for work. He meant to send you flowers from the office before he went on that out-of-town trip, but the boss called him in at the last second . . . well, you know how it goes.

What goes, my dears, is the relationship.

Romance needs nourishment and care and cosseting. That means time: time for it alone, time for you to feel loved and special, time to focus on one another. Romance is not going to thrive if you hurriedly make love in the last seven minutes before you drop dead asleep after an exhausting day at the office. It just isn't.

If you don't want a malnourished relationship on your hands, you have to set aside time for the two of you.

A friend of mine, a very big deal at a television network, finally caught a "convenient dose of Asian flu" so she could stay home for two weeks and talk to her man. Their schedules had become so crisscrossed that their relationship consisted of leaving notes for one another at the breakfast table.

"It was wonderful," she recalled. "We talked and made love and bathed together and did jigsaw puzzles. I didn't set foot outside the apartment (well, I was supposed to be ill), and we rediscovered each other just in time. Now we're deliberately making time for us. I've canceled some projects I thought I couldn't; he's turned down some trips he thought were deathly important. The world has survived, and so have we."

How much more of a lesson do the rest of us need?

Romance thrives on flattery and showmanship. Telling your man he's the handsomest guy at the party, admiring his new sports jacket, his telling you that once you walked into the room, all the other women disappeared: I mean, who objects to or gets tired of that? Showmanship is the big gesture: arriving home to find the bathtub full of roses and lilies, arranging beforehand to have the violinist play your favorite song at dinner, finding a pearl-and-gold necklace under your pillow—these are the gestures you never forget.

Quiet, understood little glances are like vitamins for romance—they help build it up! They mean you and your love inhabit a special world where only two of you know the passwords and punchlines. Of course, the knowing exchange of glances is the result of an old-fashioned, slow buildup between you. They don't develop overnight. A private world takes a little time to create.

Besides being romantic and affectionate, these secret signs can be thrilling and sexual. A friend of mine frequently meets her man at parties and social gatherings. (It's always a toss-up whether she'll show at all, with her schedule.) When she enters the room, draped in the latest madness from New York or Paris or London, her man always looks to see if she has a fresh flower tucked in her hair. If she does it means under her dress she's wearing nothing. It drives him wild.

Romantics never underestimate the power of special associations: "our restaurant," "our table," "our song." They are real and possess beautiful, evocative memories. They can be powerful aphrodisiacs.

One last word about romance: It doesn't just happen. It's not floating around in thin air looking for somewhere to settle. You have to make it happen or create the atmosphere to let it happen. It's not dependent on candlelit dinners: Romance isn't limited to the dinner hour! It doesn't have a timetable; it's a way of life.

I have literally filled the balcony adjoining our bedroom with flowers in hanging pots or earthen jars. It's a blaze of reds and yellows, blues and pinks, scarlets and purples. When I open the curtains on that sea of sensuality in the morning, I feel Leonard and I are starting the day in the right way, even though we're arguing about who will get to the exercise bike first.

I have been known to tuck romantic little notes in Leonard's briefcase and suit pockets. (Can you imagine if he handed one to a fellow bigwig at a business meeting? "Darling, about last night . . .")

I once sent him flowers, which completely baffled him (although it also charmed him). He wanted to know if I thought he'd died. A friend of mine tells me that sometimes she'll phone her man at the office and say, "Hurry home, I'm wearing something really special."

"Like what?" he says.

"Perfume," she'll reply. She just splashes herself everywhere with L'Interdit and waits for him to break down the door.

Not everyone has the time or inclination for all these romantic games, but everyone who has time for love had better find the time to feed it.

IX

Shifting Gears

• *Are You Where You Want to Be?*

All my life I've seen people shrug off their chances for success and happiness by living their lives in the condition of "if only": "If only I were in her shoes;" "If only I was thinner;" "If only I wasn't stuck here;" "If only my parents had treated me differently." Every time I hear those laments I want to shake the person and ask, "If you know that's not where you want to be, why do you stay there?"

There are enough people locked into this attitude to populate the moon! I know people who can't make up their minds in Baskin-Robbins; those thirty-one flavors give them an anxiety attack! I know others who can't change their clothes or their hairdresser without calling their therapist! I have argued with women who admit they are miserable in their present relationship but won't change it. "Oh, Micki, I couldn't bear the upheaval."

But there comes a point when we have to shift gears if we're going to grow up and get where we want to go. Despite promising circumstances, hard work, good intentions, maybe things are getting flat. Perhaps time is running out for this job, this relationship, this lifestyle. As disrupting and painful as it will be, as open to criticism as it will leave you, as frightening and draining as pursuing a new path may be, it is time to shift.

Now I know you're going to get defensive and say, "I *will* make a move; I'm just waiting for the right time." Let me share a secret with you: There *is* no right time. The time is now. If you sit around, perched like an expectant bird on the fence post, waiting for the perfect moment to act, you never will. Because perfect moments, like happy endings and Prince Charmings, belong only in fairy tales, not in real life.

That doesn't mean there aren't better times than others to make a move. If your man comes down with a killer virus and loses his job and his golf partner, it's not a good time to announce you want to quit your job and go back to school. Your plans for your life may have to be postponed until your lives together are back on track. Likewise, if his cat has just died, his horse came in last, and he's missed the million-dollar lottery by one digit, you may want to put off for twenty-four hours telling him it's over and you're leaving town.

I'm a great believer in doing something about an unhappy situation instead of waiting until it just overwhelms you and you can't act. Let's do a short quiz:

- Are you happy with your life generally?
- Do you have a rewarding job, a fulfilling and loving relationship, an acceptable lifestyle?
- Are you where you thought you'd be or planned to be at this stage of your life?
- Do you long to be living a different kind of life or to change one major part of it?

If you answered "No" to any of the first three questions and "Yes" to the last one, or if they just made you squirm a little, then it's time for changes, minor or major.

After my separation my lifestyle was no longer in keeping with the way I wanted to live. I was definitely not where I wanted to be. I knew I wanted to free myself of the suburban house, the car pool, and financial dependence. How was I to get where I wanted to be?

First step: "You need to move out of this house, Micki," I said to myself every morning for weeks.

Even though I couldn't really afford to move downtown, I bought my townhouse in the center of the city where I would be close to everything I needed to start my new life—agents, auditions, studios, friends, bank manager, theaters. When I switch gears it's usually Mack-truck style.

Next step: work. (Well, I had to pay for the foolish house, and the kids had to eat occasionally!) But I needed to bolster my confidence and find some new fields to explore, do something that was just for me.

With warnings and prophecies of doom ringing in my ears from friends and family alike, I hopped a plane to London, England, planning to have a marvelous summer meeting new people, taking an acting course, and experiencing a new kind of freedom. (When I registered the first day at the acting academy there was a note for me: "Call your mother." Mother had flown over to surprise me so I wouldn't be lonely!?! A few days later, in front of the American Express office, a BBC television crew stopped her to get an American's reaction to the latest news. "What do you think of President Nixon's resignation?" they asked as cameras and lights whirred.

"My daughter, the actress, Micki Moore, is studying at the Royal Academy," she answered. "She's a wonderful woman."

"No, no," shouted the cameraman. "I don't think you understand the question."

"No, no," responded my mother. "I don't think you understand the answer. My daughter, the actress ..." That's my mother, the press agent!)

Another summer I took an even bigger chance. Work dried up in Toronto, so I decided to try New York. (Thank goodness for kids' camps!) I set up an action plan. I got my Toronto agent to set up appointments with his New York contacts. I phoned the three people I knew in New York, looking for a place to stay. On my slim budget I was prepared to live in a hovel. A friend of a friend of one of my friends offered to share her apartment with me. I accepted, picturing a third-floor walk-up in Harlem. Was I surprised when it turned out she lived in a luxury, four-bedroom Manhattan apartment complete with housekeeper. On top of this she refused to take any money from me. And within two weeks I landed three commercials!

Oh, Micki, you're so lucky, you might say. But was it luck or the three hundred phone calls? I shifted gears for myself, I acted, and, let me tell you, sometimes when you shift gears, the earth moves!

Of course, not everyone chooses such dramatic, globe-trotting options. The shift change is usually closer to home.

I was gingerly approached once after a speaking engagement by a women who confessed she had a problem and wanted advice.

"Six months ago I started working for the first time in fifteen years," she said. "But my husband is unhappy and wants me to stay home. He's putting a lot of pressure on me. What should I do?"

"One solution," I said, "is to quit."

"But Micki," she said. "I love it. I enjoy the challenge, and I like making money. I can't go back to the way things were. I love this job."

This woman was answering her own question, really. Since going back was out of the question, the only other way was forward. She and her husband could go forward together, or she might have to face the possibility of going alone.

Naturally, this is one of the things that holds people back and makes it so difficult to shift gears—somebody always seems to get run over! You can't expect change to happen without some conflict. But you can make the changes as painless as possible for your loved ones by being honest and fair, not just with them but with your-self. (We're talking about major life changes here, not deciding to dye your hair blonde, although that, too, can be a major change, according to some mouse-into-Marilyns I've talked to!)

Part of the honesty and fairness is knowing that you really do need a change the way a fish needs water or bees need pollen, and it's not just a whim. How do you know this is real ambition and need stirring, not just indigestion or the grumblings of discontent we all feel when our neighbor waltzes in with the expensive, new dress she bought to celebrate her promotion? How do you really know?

• Reading the Signposts along the Way

I'd say it's time for you to make a move or at least recognize you might like to make a move if—

At work:

• You do your job and meet your responsibilities with ease but little satisfaction. You can't remember the last time you were challenged.
• You head off to the office (or factory or stay home facing the day's chores) with resignation, not anticipa-tion or eagerness.
• It's been eons since you sat worrying constructively about a work-related problem or issue, doodling solu-tions, mulling possible answers, your mind totally en-gaged and stimulated by the possibility of finding a solution.
• You passionately envy the work of others.
• You passionately resent the work or careers of others.
• You long to have something attainable that your work doesn't provide, like fame or more money or national recognition. Too much time spent in wish-fulfillment fantasies is a big indication that your work is uninspir-ing, not challenging, and that you could do more.

In your relationship:

• You and your mate rarely talk to each other except to remind the other to put out the garbage or take the dog to the vet. There's no hostility, but there's no communication either.

• You have separate interests and are beginning to form separate groups of friends and spend more and more time away from one another.

• Your sex life is just a memory, or worse, a chore.

• Your work, clothes, kids, house, bridge club is more important to you than your mate.

• You don't care how you look when he's around. Any old rag of a housecoat will do for him, although you wouldn't open the door to the meter-reader dressed that way.

• You don't bother to argue with him anymore.

• You can't remember the last time the two of you shared a secret kiss or hug in the kitchen away from the prying eyes of the kids.

• You dream constantly about other men—movie stars, your doctor, the delivery boy, a mystery man glimpsed on a passing subway train.

• You've taken your dreams one step further and are actually having an affair and hating yourself for it.

• You've taken your dreams one step further and are actually having an affair and loving yourself for it. "It fills up the afternoons," one woman told me.

• You long to try new things but don't suggest them, because he won't be interested. He'll denigrate any new interest—"Why the hell do you want to take jewelry design at night school, Laura? Why don't you take something useful or just stay home?"

You:

• You have two hundred diet books in the house and are still twenty pounds overweight.

• You hate your hair, your shape, your wardrobe, your

feet, your complexion, your walk.

• You'd love to pursue a career in advertising but are too fed up with life in the typing pool to find the energy to go to night classes.

• You're so bored with your household routine that you're considering joining an urban guerilla group to break the monotony.

• You hate your former best friend for going back to school and getting a great job.

And on the positive side, maybe it's time to shift gears if:

• You feel a flood of ambition, desire, and confidence when more difficult jobs and higher positions are mentioned.

• You experience a burst of assurance about your relationship, and you feel ready to take it to the next step.

• Circumstances change (your grown-up children leave home), and you see this as an opportunity rather than a loss.

Signposts can be both positive and negative, and it's hard to say which has the most impact—the negative-into-positive, probably. You know, the kind of thing where you decide, like Howard Beal in the film *Network*, that "I'm mad as hell and I'm not going to take it anymore." Then you go do something about it.

That's when the nightmares really begin—when you, heart and soul, are taking a risk.

• How Willing Are You to Take the Risk?

"Micki, you are crazy."

At times it seems my life has been peppered with that line; it's come from my father, husband, kids, friends, even Leonard.

Micki, you are crazy to keep working when you don't have to.

Micki, you are crazy to dress up in a chicken costume for that commercial.

Micki, you are crazy to fly off to London with so little money and knowing no one.

Micki, you are crazy to ride in that parade down Yonge Street wearing three large spangles and a smile.

Micki, you are crazy to think you are going to do anything special with your life or leave any mark on the world.

Micki, you are crazy to think of doing whatever it is you're thinking of doing—think of the risk.

I do, and let me tell all those doomsayers who wanted to run my life: They were wrong. Risks are worth taking. From taking risks come the rewards.

Life is risk. Being born is a risk. Crossing the road for the first time on your way to kindergarten is a risk. Riding your bicycle in city traffic is a risk. Going to camp, learning to swim, your first date, your final exam—they're all risks. Your first job, first marriage—loaded with risk. How much risk can one chicken costume be after that? There's almost nothing you can do in life from making angel food cake to making love that doesn't involve risk.

Risk taking is one of the most exhilarating sports I've played. So why is everyone so uptight about the extra risks life tosses at you, like leaving your job in a bank to join the circus or sailing around the world in a dinghy or falling in love with a mad poet?

If you want a snug, safe, cocooned world where you can sit like a stuffed trout, then don't make a move. Don't change a thing. Don't take a teeny step forward. You're safe—and "on hold." One of life's golden, maybe platinum rules, is: No risk—no change—no growth.

But nobody takes a major risk in life without some stomach-churning fear. If we weren't weak with terror it wouldn't be a risk, would it? I talked to a television commentator who was about to jump stations, and he was completely melting with fear.

"I'm leaving an established network to work for a small station, because I think I need the artistic freedom it gives me," he said. "But when I think of what I'm doing in terms of my future career if this doesn't work out . . ." For this man time had come. He had a choice: to stay where he was, as contented as a cow, and moo away the next thirty working years of his life or to move, take the risk of becoming someone bigger, better, more satisfied, more alive.

Some of the fear of risk taking is banished if you approach it in the same spirit you approach skill building—one skill on top of another, remember? Well, try one risk on top of another. For example: Say you're dying to open your own boutique. It's a big risk; you need capital, experience, buyer expertise, marketing, advertising—a billion things that novice you doesn't know. But you can cut the risk by breaking your dream down into a series of "mini-risks": first working in a boutique to get the feel of the business, meeting some buyers and designers, trying for independent commissions from home, taking on partners to split the losses (and profits, of course). Risk needn't overwhelm you. You can make it manageable.

Risk is not a luxury reserved for the imperious, bold, and fearless. It's for everyone, like good sex and raspberries out of season. You need two realizations to start: You've been taking risks since day one, and to live you have to act. I'm not suggesting that all of you start abandoning jobs, marriages, children, friends, and all the anchors of your lives just because they are familiar. But in most areas of your life you know when you're just coasting and when you should risk something to reach your best.

An excellent definition of success—one that has yellowed with age on my fridge door—is: "Success is being everything you're capable of being." If you're not all that, maybe it's time to explore why not.

• What If My Need to Change Threatens Our Relationship?

Of course, the problem with changing is that not everyone changes at the same rate or even at all. What happens when you feel the need to spring out of the cocoon like a beautiful butterfly and he's happy wriggling along like a caterpillar? What if his response to your brave new self is: "I don't like it. Change back, or I'm leaving."

Well, my dear, having set you up for all this, I'm going to tell you now that if that happens, you're on your own. Only you can gauge the depth of your feelings for him, for the old you, the new you, your ambitions, your dreams, and what you stand to lose. I don't have to spend long winter nights without Norman just because I thought I wanted to give up computer programming and be a tightrope dancer. On the other hand, I don't have to lie next to snoring Norman and dream with an aching heart of that dancer's pink-and-silver costume and the bright lights and the applause.

An actress friend of mine who was going through these agonies told me, "I had one chance in a thousand of getting that part, and Ray was enraged about my taking off for a month to California. He said, 'If you go, it's forever.' But I had to. I'd have regretted not trying the rest of my life. It was a calculated risk." Unfortunately (this does happen, dreamers, don't forget), Elizabeth didn't get her part in the sexy soap, and she came back to an empty apartment.

"Ray moved out just like he threatened he would," she said. "But I still don't regret taking the risk. What kind of relationship would we have had if I'd felt blackmailed into giving up something I desperately wanted just to cajole him out of one of his moods?"

We all have to take and face our risks just a little bit with shoulders squared and knuckles bared. Nobody wants to be Indiana Jones hanging from a rope bridge or the Human Fly scaling the Wrigley Building, but it feels like that sometimes. We all have anxiety, but as someone once said, "Everyone has butterflies. The trick is to teach them to fly in formation."

I've learned that one way to face risks is to welcome them, because they are a chance to learn and grow and profit from experience. You've all heard that expression: "If only I knew then what I know now." Well, you can't know or get the experience of life without living a little.

But I have found (in dark corners, crouching behind chairs) people who deliberately plan their lives to avoid risks because they fear the consequences, even if one of the consequences is success. They don't want the big promotion with all its extra responsibility, pressure, and stress. They don't want to fall in love and risk the pain. They don't want to share themselves or be consumed with passion.

They have a point. Relationships are the riskiest ventures of all. You want to live together; he doesn't. He wants to get married; you don't. Even voicing what you really want in a relationship is a risk, because it lays the groundwork for arguments and ultimatums—and maybe Splitsville. I think sending Leonard that chocolate chip cookiegram was a risk, but it's crumbs (sorry, couldn't resist) compared to truly fearless risk-takers like Lindsay. She risked her marriage when she told her husband she was no longer sure she wanted to live so closely together: together, yes, but not so much like a three-legged race. "I want a couple of nights a week to myself to do what I want to do," she told him. Alone.

Of course, like all husbands and lovers, David immediately conjured up visions of her bar hopping with the girls, hot discos, traveling sales reps, and silver-tongued ad men. But he didn't say no (or not very loudly). What Lindsay did with her nights off was quite different from David's x-rated fears. She went to art classes and is now a successful illustrator of children's books.

I have made my share of mistakes in relationships, but one thing I've learned for sure and can save you the trouble of finding out the painful way: Intimacy is destroyed by lack of change. That same plodding groove that the two of you are wearing out together is wearing out your relationship, too. You are yoked together like beasts of burden instead of being joined in love.

The green young man of twenty must develop into the questing man of thirty and assured man of forty. The insecure woman of twenty needs to blossom into the confident thirty-year-old and successful, accomplished forty-year-old. Why, then, when couples are growing along together, do they so often grow apart? (Leonard says this makes me sound like a gardener.)

Too often one partner in the relationship is changing like a chameleon, and the other is sitting there like a rock. "My marriage is perfect, why should I change it?" is something I've heard a lot. Change for the sake of change, no, but change is usually for the sake of growth. What your nonchanging partner is doing is putting you in a time machine where he (or she) can freeze the perfect moment—like freeze-dried coffee or frozen raspberries—and stay in control. But no one can stop exploration, expression, and growth. All they do is create a lot of resentment, anger, and unhappiness instead.

One of my neighbors was in just that situation with her husband. "Lorne wanted me to be at forty the same sweet, pliable young woman I was at twenty," she said. "He hated it when I learned to drive, hated it when I went on the Pill, hated it when I got a job after the kids were in school.

"He had an eternal vision of me in a little white blouse with a Peter Pan collar and a ribbon in my hair waiting for him in the swing-seat on the porch. In the end I left him with his vision. My reality had far surpassed it."

It is just the opposite for my friend Jane. "John and I have grown up together," this forty-eight-year-old urban planner said. "Our friends have changed, our interests have expanded, we're both more independent yet also interdependent. He's never resented my success, and I've always welcomed his."

But in the beginning, I asked her, what gave you the courage to take the risks before you knew John would be so supportive?

Her answer inspired me, and I hope it will you.

"I believed in what I was doing," she said. "I didn't have to debate with myself over whether it was right or wrong. I had faith in myself, and that conviction helped John to believe in me, too."

Actresses always long for great, dramatic stage entrances, but in life I've found that knowing how to make a memorable exit is just as valuable.

Dare we talk about that now?

• Letting Go

When my marriage was breaking up my husband said, "You're driving me out." And I answered him, "But you're driving me to drive you out." Both statements were true; nobody was at fault. All I could do during that difficult time was comfort myself with the words of one of my favorite authors, Nathaniel Branden, that "ending a relationship doesn't mean that someone has failed; it means only that someone has changed, perhaps for the better."

Now here is something else to write in icing on the top of your next cake: "Nothing is forever." As you move through life you will have to give up or be given up by parents, friends, men, children. You may have to leave homes and places you love. And people you adore. Sometimes you and your loved one are on separate merry-go-rounds, and nothing will get you together. When I was going through my divorce, I changed the words from "letting go" to "starting over." It puts the emphasis on future promise, adventure, and opportunity. Yes, it is the end of one relationship, but the future is alive with new possibilities, and that's where to concentrate your aims, energies, and passions.

While you're in the process of letting go, you'll be whirling with mixed emotions of hope and fear, anxiety, resentment, anger, misery. You'll be convinced this only happens to you, that nobody else has suffered in this way; you'll get a sudden fit of "mea culpa" in which everything is your fault, and you'll want to crawl back on your hands and knees to patch things up (except you won't, because your best friend will chain you to the gatepost). When you're finally free of the pain of letting go, you will view your future with renewed hope and expectation.

Now, having got you really excited about leaving the dishes, the vacuuming, and Albert still trying to stoke up the barbeque, a word of caution and common sense. Don't let go easily. Make fate pry your fingers off the bedpost if you think the relationship has a ghost of a chance.

It's wrong to walk away simply because it's easier than staying. It's wrong and cowardly to leave because you're rather bored but don't want to talk it out, and it's easier to slip away in the night without a word like a teenage runaway. It's wrong when there is a flicker of love that may be rekindled, when there is any reasonable hope for a change in the other person, when the joy or contentment outweighs the pain even by a fraction. Only when you're overwhelmed by suffering and the happiness is completely snuffed out is it time to let go. If that's the case, be like the old Prussian general who, when asked what direction his army would move in, replied gallantly, "There is only one way: forward."

Onward, then.

• Strategies for Moving Ahead

You're moving into high gear. Ready?

• Acknowledge to yourself, out loud if you have to, that after much soul-searching and careful weighing of pros and cons, you are taking a step toward a brighter, more positive future.

• Accept that there will be difficulties and setbacks along the way. Knowing this will help to give you the strength to deal with them.

• Map out your game plan in detail so you know where you're going and why.

• Be prepared to put in hours and effort at first for very little reward.

• If you've left a relationship behind, think positively about what the future holds. It's a mysterious voyage charged with excitement. Don't dwell on your romantic past with your ex-man; your wounded pride and imagination are painting a black-and-white relationship in technicolor.

• Realize it won't be easy to carve a new life and that those closest to you—parents, friends, spouse—are often the first to make you feel guilty, foolish, and doubtful. You're not. You're taking a risk, making a change, making a move that you need as much as your lungs need oxygen.

• Be prepared for a major catastrophe somewhere, lurking in the wings. The path of true independence, like that of true love, doesn't run smooth.

• Don't expect overnight miracles. Everything worth having is worth laboring for. Committed relationships are better than one-night stands; a cultivated career success is more fulfilling than an overnight fluke.

• Don't let others get at you with: "If only you'd listened to me" when things are in a bumpy patch. Not trying is the only failure in life. Trying, risking, moving on is always a step toward success.

• Once you're there or comfortable with your new flight path, take some time to enjoy it. Share it with others; revel in it. Your hand has shaped your future and will continue to do so.

Just as life is full of risks, it is also full of price tags.

There are no free lunches, no free rides. So don't expect success to come cheap.

Take the risk, make the move, because you have to: You have to be challenged, pushed, stretched to tap every ounce of precious ability. You need to push yourself the way an athlete does, knowing there will be tough days and hurdles along the way. But never doubt it's worth it.

If I'd held on to my doubts and misgivings, I'd still be a suburban housewife with a Southern accent as thick as wallpaper paste, still dreaming and discontent.

If I'd given in to the bruises and socked jaws on the way up, I would have retired to a trailer home in Florida before my kids were out of high school.

If I'd said no to every opportunity and every risk life threw at me, I'd be bored and lonely with fifteen cats and a parakeet today.

So, lady, set down your overloaded backpack of anxiety, doubts, and fears, and get ready to fly!

X

Taking Flight

• A Man's Gotta Do What a Man's Gotta Do—And So Does a Woman!

Well, this is it! The moment when your toes leave terra firma and you spread your wings and soar.

Well, isn't it?

Don't worry, I'm not going to send you out there alone. Take a friend with you, the same one I take. I discovered her in this quote: "One's best friend is in the mirror." Once you know that, there are really no dragons you can't go out there and slay.

But what kind of person are you, you who are about to launch yourself on the unsuspecting world? What kind of woman wants to make her mark, seek out adventure, and create a life for herself? Look in the mirror at that woman brimming with confidence, self-assured, self-reliant, and full of belief in herself and what she wants from life.

Knowing what you want, striving, sharing, working hard—life is so rich it seems impossible not to get some of the goodness if you go after it.

And your dreams are pointing the way. Your dreams are as individual as your thumbprint, so don't let anyone tell you they are "wrong," "crazy," or "impractical." Dreams can't be controlled. Let them fly where they will. Let them tell you what is important in your world; then seek it out and fill your world with it.

227

We don't question a man's right to follow his dream. A man's gotta do what a man's gotta do. So do you—which is follow your convictions and be the best you can be.

There will be competition; there will be setbacks. But you are a mature, intelligent, questing adult in control of her own life. Unless you're in the army, don't take orders! Since you are the number-one person in your world, only you can decide what your world is going to be like. To borrow from Leo Buscaglia, "You take the paintbrush, you choose your colors, you paint your paradise, and then you live in it."

Having puffed you up with all this, let me add a couple of notes of caution: Don't let too many daydreams of international stardom and four-hundred-acre horse farms swarming with Arabian princes drain all your energy when you could be doing something real in the here and now. Your dreams, for all their luxuriance and inspiration, have got to be wings you can wear. At forty it's a little late to decide to be a ballerina. And eighteen is too young to decide you'll be happy with one man, one dog, two babies, and a split-level in suburbia forever.

Make sure you are not trying to live someone else's dream. If your mother dreams of you becoming a concert pianist while you want to be an Olympic marathoner, let Mom take the music lessons—you've got to run. If your husband decides you should both give up your law practices and buy a sheep farm in the Hebrides, tell him to write when he's got enough wool for a designer sweater! The easiest thing in the world to be is you. The hardest is trying to be a character dreamed up by someone else. All you can say to those who would mold you in their image is: "That is not me. This is me, with these talents, abilities, characteristics, and these faults, quirks, idiosyncrasies."

Don't despair if you feel right now that you can hardly change the TV channel, let alone your life. Everyone has moments when they are charged with almost divine power to get what they want. Maybe yours just hasn't happened yet, or you've been so caught up in the niggling business of everyday life that you haven't left room for dreams to grow. Your time will come if you let it. It's a time when you feel flooded with strength, spurred on by ambition and desire; you're surging on power. (Leonard says now I've given up gardening and am into electrical engineering!)

Keep this thought with you on the road to success and self-fulfillment: Never feel for a moment that you don't deserve it. Just the fact that you are an individual, a good person brimming with unique abilities, entitles you to a huge helping of the fine things in life—love, friendship, and personal success. But all the success formulas in the world, corked up in old champagne bottles and delivered in a Rolls on your next birthday, are meaningless unless you know you're entitled. In this respect there are no harnesses, halters, ropes, or chains but the ones you forge.

You have a life to live, not just as someone's daughter (although that is a blessed relationship), not just as somebody's lover and wife (although that is abundant in its rewards), not just as a mother (although nothing matches the commitment and joy of children), and not just as a dear friend (although the rewards of mutual sharing are precious indeed).

But in addition to—not instead of—all these connections, there must be some time, some space, something just for you. You're entitled to a chance to reveal what you are about, to shine, to show what's in your heart, wherever your talents may lie.

You've gotta do what you've gotta do. Believe it, and you will!

• It's All Out There—Go Get It!

Any wheeler-dealer financier can tell you that you have to spend money to make money. Bank notes or emotions, it's the same—you have to put out feelings to get some back. It's the same if you're reaching for success: You have to put out and risk to get your rewards. If just thinking about it makes you shiver with timidity, consider: If you had one week left to live, how would you spend it? Not scrubbing floors, cleaning the kids' shoes, tap-tap-tapping in the typing pool, or turning down a party because you have nothing to wear. If you had to compact all your living dreams into one week, what would you do? But you don't. You've got the rest of your life. Longer than a week, but shorter than you think, so get going.

Here's one more of Micki's checklists to help you get ready for your right flight path:

- If you believe you can't do it, you won't be able to.
- If you believe you haven't got what it takes, you won't have what it takes.
- If you believe everyone out there is brighter, more beautiful, luckier, and more talented than you are, they will be.
- If you believe your man will leave you for someone else, he will.
- If you believe you aren't really entitled to some of the greater things in life your heart aches for, you won't get them.

BUT

- If you believe you can do anything you want, or learn to do it, or at least are willing to try for the satisfaction of giving it your best shot, you will do it.
- If you believe you've got what it takes but you need a little more time, experience, and training and are willing to take action, you'll have it, because you've got the spirit.
- If you believe your man will live with you in a loving, rewarding relationship for as long as the two of you keep loving and trying and working at it, he will, and it will work.

• If you believe you deserve some of the golden spoils of life and are willing to go after them, you'll get them.

Now, before you rush out and set the world on fire, may I add one more thing: Of all the wonderful qualities you possess, the ones that will see you across the finish line are *persistence* and *perseverance*. I know you're talented, capable, and ambitious. I know you have dreams and confidence and spirit. So did hundreds of women who are now rocking on front porches murmuring, "I wish, I wish . . . "

The world is crammed with talented, educated, advantaged people doing nothing and going nowhere, because they didn't have the gumption to stick to it. That, of course, won't be you.

One last word (I promise): The purpose of all this energy and effort is to bring you happiness.

So you can create your own vision of success and fulfill every promise to yourself.

So you can be a woman of character, not just some character's woman!

So you can look forward to your ninetieth birthday with no regrets, just wonderful memories of all the fun and foolish things you did, the wild risks you took, the great love you knew, the deep satisfaction and pleasure with life you felt, whether you were making millions in the corporate maelstrom or making muffins for your beloved family.

Be true to yourself and your dreams when you are making a life for yourself, making bread, making love, or making the people close to you happy. Make a place for yourself, a mark in the world, some sign that you were here—then you are truly *making it!*

The Author

For six years, Micki Moore was the interviewer/host of CITY-TV's talk show "You're Beautiful", originating in Toronto and syndicated throughout Canada. Ms. Moore has now resumed her former career as actress and writer and continues to do television interviewing.

Ms. Moore is a graduate of Ohio State University, where she majored in Radio and Television Arts. She studied at the Royal Academy of Dramatic Art (RADA) in London and at the Actor's Studio. She lives in Toronto.

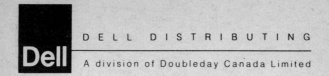

*Watch for these great paperbacks coming
this year:*

Murder With Muskets	John Reeves
Additive Alert	Linda Pim
Pirates and Outlaws	Harold Horwood and Ed Butts
Don't Bank On It	Alix Granger
Murder Before Matins	John Reeves

Dell Distributing is a new paperback
program publishing books for all interests in
Canada. Look for **Dell Distributing** paperbacks wherever you find Dell paperbacks like
these bestsellers:

Thy Neighbor's Wife	Gay Talese
Men In Love	Nancy Friday
Go For It!	Dr. Irene Kassorla
The Feminine Mystique	Betty Friedan

Dell GET A DELL PAPERBACK FREE...

Take a few moments to check off your answers to the following questions. Have your reply **postmarked by June 1, 1986** and we'll send you a brand new DELL PAPERBACK, absolutely free!

1. Are you ☐ MALE? ☐ FEMALE?

2. What is the highest level of education you have completed?
   ☐ SOME HIGH SCHOOL OR LESS
   ☐ HIGH SCHOOL GRADUATE
   ☐ SOME COLLEGE/UNIVERSITY/OTHER POST-SECONDARY
   ☐ GRADUATED COLLEGE/UNIVERSITY/OTHER POST-SECONDARY
   ☐ POST-GRADUATE STUDIES

3. In which age group are you?
   ☐ UNDER 18 YEARS OLD   ☐ 35–49
   ☐ 18–24   ☐ 50–64
   ☐ 25–34   ☐ 65 OR OVER

4. Please indicate the best description of your job.
   ☐ STUDENT   ☐ OWNER/MANAGERIAL
   ☐ LABOURER OR SEMI-SKILLED   ☐ HOMEMAKER
   ☐ SKILLED   ☐ RETIRED
   ☐ CLERICAL OR SALES   ☐ UNEMPLOYED
   ☐ PROFESSIONAL OR TECHNICAL

   What is the average number of paperbacks you buy in a month?
   ☐ FEWER THAN ONE A MONTH   ☐ 5 TO 6 A MONTH
   ☐ 1 A MONTH   ☐ 7 TO 11 A MONTH
   ☐ 2 TO 4 A MONTH   ☐ 12 OR MORE A MONTH

   Which kind(s) of paperbacks do you usually buy?
   ☐ POLITICAL/SPY THRILLERS   ☐ SPORTS NON-FICTION
   ☐ SUPERNATURAL THRILLERS   ☐ TRUE CRIME
   ☐ MYSTERIES   ☐ CURRENT EVENTS
   ☐ MODERN ROMANCES   ☐ SELF-IMPROVEMENT/SELF-HELP
   ☐ HISTORICAL ROMANCES   ☐ HISTORY
   ☐ WAR FICTION   ☐ EXPOSE
   ☐ "BESTSELLER-LIST" FICTION   ☐ BUSINESS
   ☐ OTHER FICTION   ☐ "BESTSELLER-LIST" NON-FICTION
   ☐ BIOGRAPHIES   ☐ SCIENCE FICTION

   Please underline the book description above which you feel best describes this book.

8. Did you see or hear any advertising for this book before you purchased it?
   ☐ YES   ☐ NO   ☐ DON'T KNOW
   If you checked yes, where?
   ☐ RADIO   ☐ MAGAZINES
   ☐ TELEVISION   ☐ BILLBOARDS
   ☐ BUS AND SUBWAY POSTERS

9. Did you see or hear any reviews for this book before you purchased it?
   ☐ YES   ☐ NO   ☐ DON'T KNOW
   If you checked yes, where?
   ☐ RADIO   ☐ NEWSPAPER
   ☐ TELEVISION   ☐ MAGAZINE

10. Did you see or hear any author interviews or other promotion for this
    book before you purchased it?
    ☐ YES   ☐ NO   ☐ DON'T KNOW
    If you checked yes, where?
    ☐ RADIO   ☐ NEWSPAPER
    ☐ TELEVISION   ☐ MAGAZINE

11. Did someone personally recommend this book to you?
    ☐ YES   ☐ NO

12. Did you purchase this book the first time you saw it in a retail outlet?
    ☐ YES   ☐ NO

13. Please indicate where you purchased this book.
    ☐ DEPARTMENT STORE   ☐ DRUG STORE
    ☐ CONVENIENCE STORE   ☐ STATIONERY STORE
    ☐ AIRPORT, BUS OR TRAIN TERMINAL   ☐ BOOKSTORE
    ☐ SUPERMARKET

OPTIONAL QUESTION: Please indicate the bracket which is closest to your
estimate of the total gross income of all members of your household.
    ☐ UNDER $15,000 A YEAR
    ☐ $15,000 TO $29,999 A YEAR
    ☐ $30,000 OR MORE A YEAR

HAVE YOU ANSWERED ALL THE QUESTIONS ON THE OTHER SIDE?

To get your free DELL PAPERBACK, please cut out and mail this page today.
DELL PAPERBACKS GIVEAWAY, 105 Bond St., Toronto, Ont. M5B 1Y3. Be sure
to include your name and address in the space provided. Thank You.

NAME _____

ADDRESS _____

POSTAL CODE _____